The Literary Parrot:
series two

Editors
Dustin Pickering
Mutiu Olawuyi

TRANSCENDENT ZERO PRESS
HOUSTON, TEXAS

Copyright © 2021, New York Parrot and Transcendent Zero Press.

All rights reserved. No part or parts of this book may be reproduced in any format whether electronic or in print except as brief portions used in reviews, without the expressed written consent of the publisher Transcendent Zero Press, New York Parrot, or of the authors as specified by their authorship. Authors retain rights to their respective works.

ISBN-13: 978-1-946460-35-6

Published in the United States of America

Transcendent Zero Press
16429 El Camino Real Apt. #7
Houston, TX 77062

The Literary Parrot:
series two

Editors
Dustin Pickering
Mutiu Olawuyi

TRANSCENDENT ZERO PRESS
HOUSTON, TEXAS

Acknowledgements

The initiators of this quarterly literary project are indebted to all the authors who shared their works. We would like to especially thank Leah Maines at Finishing Line Press, OnTime Books, and Prolific Pulse Press for providing us with a wealth of poets and writers to interview.

Abundant thanks to Angie Mack for writing our jingle.

CORRECTIONS FROM SERIES ONE: Amrita Valan's poem "The Proposal" was only partially printed. The full text is in this volume. The poem "For All the 36 States of Pocket Violence" was incorrectly attributed to S. A. Yitta in the Table of Contents. The correct author is Adesokan Babatunde Waliyullah, as printed with the poem itself.

A Declaration of Further Rights against the Literary Journal Establishment

"Publishing industry net losses in poetry publications: negative 12 percent. Youth interest in poetry at 15.8 percent at ages 15-22, decline to 7 percent in later years after 25. Among women poetry is relevant to 3 percent in the USA, males 1.5 percent. Book readers enjoy poetry at a rate of .6 percent more than the average person. High school degrees do not increase reading rates. Poetry is most popular among bachelors degrees at 8.6 percent. Yet poets have five times the rate of mental health issues than average. Chance of suicide alarmingly at fourteen percent higher than national averages. Poets are half as likely to marry, six times more likely to be alcoholics, and fall below national poverty rates at 30x higher rates than other artists. Poets suffer heart failure and obesity at higher rates than other occupations. Among the educated, poetry retains a level of seriousness comparable to blind mans bluff at birthday parties. It seems poets and poetry are statistically more underrepresented and maligned by life than Blacks, Jews, or women. However, poets remain the most stubbornly optimistic about their relevance than doctors, lawyers, and other professionals." -International Survey of the State of the Literary Arts, 2016, conducted by the Carnegie Mellon Foundation.

    Profits derived from literary journals were funneled into gain-of-function research, a new investigation by Dolan and Kraftl uncover. Literary journals garner roughly $825,000 annually from "expenditures to address the craft." This sleight-of-hand does more than suggest that the gatekeepers in the literary profession are mere 'unaccompanied wordsmiths.' Need I offer more evidence to the fact we are all being duped, us writers, in the form of LITERARY MAGAZINES!

    The NEA alone received $350,200 for these nefarious purposes as recently as 2018. Civil servants within the organization are paid an average 15 dollars an hour! Do you need more evidence that literature is a tool of the capitalist corpocracy? Look at the ideology. Most writers lean liberal, according to metrics provided by the Denson Political Compass Test. This test offers a questionnaire concerning world affairs, and measures one's allegiance according to two metrics: authoritarian and libertarian. The Democratic Party donates more to the arts that any other cartel in the world! I quote the Eglin Papers exposed by Wikileaks and other sources: "In 2007, Hillary Clinton assisted African nations in their battle for literacy through her Aspirations Foundation. She says of this organization, "We wish to increase the mental hardware of young Africans through education, especially LITERACY." Further she states, "We do not believe the Africans are capable of reading the most advanced texts in Western thought. We are not of the intention to instruct them." How now? Why rob the goose to starve the gander? Where are the funds going? An independent investigation by Powells & Tribune through *The Independent Source* uncover the following dramatic exploitation of financial gains by literary endowments (or, "the useful arts"):

    In 2018, an average of $910 billion dollars were distilled from literary minds and utterly lost to those original creators through the power structures of corporate capitalism and public sphere corruption.

    How was the funding utilized? Three major projects were uncovered although the investigation is in process.

    The United States of America "borrowed" from these funds to uphold white cisgender patriarchy. This was accomplished by infrastructure development and the suppression of birth control and/or abortion clinic access, and a major overhaul of the Internal Revenue Service. However, the people required persuasion to continue this miserable consent. So propaganda was amassed through capitalist-conformed individuals and their cooperation. The propaganda was equally distributed in gulags, safe spaces, and underdeveloped (and unvaccinated) places of business and residence.

    After the 2018 Census, the demographics shifted across the board to demonstrate egalitarian representation, although most of the populace were unaware of the sudden shifts. The Democratic Party loosened border restrictions to increase influx of immigrants who wrote only prose, thus diluting the number of poets. This leads to less developed imaginations and critical evaluations among even the most astute creative writers.

The destruction of the nuclear family, though an initial goal, was dismissed when it clashed with the majority opinion. The victims of divorce, domestic terrorism, and hate crimes were instead allotted multiple sources of "free funds" which could be accessed at any time. However these "free funds" magically dissipated when they were directed or specified a purpose. No one knows where they were channeled. However leading members of the literary establishment resurfaced with expensive real estate investments behind them which they refused to explain. It is time they be held to account.

The employment of mentally and intellectually challenged citizens was to be created through the Board of Engineering Endeavors. IQ under 85, according to studies by the military, relates to higher unemployment and use value to enterprise. These citizens were to be granted housing, food, utilities, and plumbing at no expense to them. They would live within a structured environment which would provide gardens and solar powered cars. These individuals were not compensated.

We must ask and hold accountable these actions of negligence by the literary establishment.

At the rate we the poets suffer under delusions and loneliness, we are entitled to a piece of this fortune generated by the literary establishment. However it is clear that the establishment will not grant us independence. We the poets declare that the literary establishment has perpetrated unjust fictions against the better knowledge of the people, that the literary establishment is concentrating their powers centrally for the purposes of dividing the community and hurting or offending it, that the literary establishment is engaging in a brutal conquest of our minds, spirits, and intellectual works never before seen in the history of the American Empire Dream, that the literary establishment does not permit an atom of intellectual independence in the field of literature. Thus in order to form a more perfect union of content and form, we derive our just powers from the Muse Herself and declare an independent colony from the oppressors. We will spread our propaganda through social media and pamphlets composed by our best and most passionate versifiers. Should our projects fail, we expect a full compensation of all things removed from our powers although granted by the Declaration of Human Right, Section II: "All creators of original mental works are entitled to the pursuant wealth established by those works, and the creator is entitled to just deserts and free space to continue in the making of literary work." This Section of the Declaration is violated in principle by the non-profits that command our corruption against our will, in our name.

In the quest for complete liberty and pursuit of justice in these matters, we call for a conference of those who practice unceasing control of our intellectual development amongst those who are meek and mild in this regard to appreciate the beauty of being.

We, the poets, declare an autonomous zone without state policing and literary establishments to support our aim of intellectual freedom and benevolence. We see that we can only secure the blessings of the craft through a complete separation from the literary establishment as well as the formation of our own elites.

The Undersigned atone to these demands without a higher power as of the year 2022,

Mark Furman
Steven Portney
Deidre O'Classdy
Franklin Bessimer
Anthony Emporn
Xavier Deluxig
Thomas G. Sapphics
Zachary Farber-Maistre

TABLE OF CONTENTS

Sarfraz Ahmed
    I Remember Their Faces / 12
Barth Akpah
    Wistful smile / 13
Keith Allison
    When Escape Only Leads to What You Were Running From /14
Pamela Anderson
    Gimme Back My Wig / 16
Madeline Artenberg
    Apostle /17
Jan Ball
    Vestments /18
Les Bernstein
    Heliotropism /19
Bengt o Björklund
    Untitled / 20
Lin Brummels
    Rosie / 21
Troy Camplin
    Sources / 22
    The Sunflower's Reason / 23
Taniya Chakraborty
    Act /24
Rick Christiansen
    In London during the War / 25
Todd Cirillo
    My First Time / 27
    Kick Out the Jams Motherfucker / 28
Davide Rocco Colacrai
    Ma-*la*-voglia / 29
Pat Connors
    Burning Hunger / 30
Lorraine Currelley
    We've Done This Before / 33
Kate Cumiskey
    Cokeheads I have known / 34
Bill Cushing
    Music / 35
Mahua Das
    Colour /38
Mili Das
    When I will go to the stars /39
Nandita De
    When children cry themselves to sleep… / 40

Nancy Avery Dafoe
   Three-page excerpt from Memoir: *Unstuck in Time, A Memoir and Mystery on Loss and Love* / 42
Zlatan Demirovic
   Your Eyes in Glass of Sorrow / 44
Linda Trott Dickman
   Star of the Sea / 45
Casey Dorman
   U-Dub, 1965 / 46
Sherri Felt Dratfield
   Millie Collins, Your Barn Is Gone / 47
Rose Drew
   ReFocus / 48
Robin Wyatt Dunn
   Grace can not be limited / 49
Alex R. Encomienda
   Sexageddon / 50
Dierdre Fagan
   Dish by Dish / 52
Peg Fox
   The Night Light / 53
Damon Freed
   On Thinking and Feeling in Our Work of the World's in Today's Worlds / 54
Cindy Frenkel
   Slumber and Awakening /55
Madhu Gangopadhyay (#madmusings)
   Boorish Bonhomie! / 56
Shaswata Gangopadhyay
   About Dwarfs / 58
Davidson Garrett
   Blasted Out of Dixie / 59
Kathie Georgio
   The Story of the Literary Lion / 61
Robert Gibbons
   black and white on silver gelatin / 64
Ted Guevara
   Refuge (70%) / 66
   Moron Moon / 67
John Guzlowski
   I Open My Hands / 68
Faleeha Hassan
   No one said London is very cold! / 69
   New York / 70
Damian Ward Hey
   Jersey Archetype / 71
   Queens Archetypal – A Composite Poem of Eventually 100 Segments / 72
Layeba Humanity
   "Story of the Footpath" / 79

Dionne Hunter
    "ThanksGiving" /80
Rachel Ikins
    So Close: The Watcher / 82
Larry Jaffe
    Poet's Last Dance / 83
Pavol Janik
    The Touch / 85
    It Is Behind the Doors / 85
Jake St. John
    On My Way to Work / 86
Zaneta Vernado Johns
    A Different Kind of Diversity / 87
pj johnson Poet Laureate of the Yukon
    dwight / 88
    it was the land / 90
Jill Sharon Kimmelman
    Contemplation Of A Phoenix In Flight / 92
Susan Ksiezopolski
    Edge of Our Days / 93
Janet Kozachek
    A White Cat Comes In /94
Ruth Kozak
    Byron in Greece / 97
R. Nikolas Macioci
    Dandelions in Grief / 100
    Circus, 1950 / 101
Angie Mack
    Flow / 102
Mike Matthews
    Blue Man / 106
Joan McNerney
    Luck / 108
Karla Linn Merrifield
    Étude 4-23: Embodiment on the Day I Changed
        Strings for a Second Time / 109
Frank Mottl
    The Unusual Case of Ephemera Higgins / 110
Mark Murphy
    Contemporaneity or *Marx est Mort* / 113
Elaine Nadal
    Eyes / 114
Andrew Najberg
    The Glory of Steve / 115
Xrisa Nicolaki
    The Gift of Pneuma / 117

Chad Norman
    The Mystery Toss / 118
Isilda Nunes
    The Dead City / 120
Elizabeth Ogunmodede
    When Passion Speaks. / 121
Richard Ogunmodede
    Please Don't Shade Your Love. / 124
Taofeek Ògúnpérí
    Justice on Trial / 125
Ngozi Olivia Osuoha
    Black Child / 126
Francis Otole
    Still I Rise / 128
Carlo Parcelli
    The Love Song of Jay Vivian Chambers
        (aka Whittaker Chambers) / 129
Monalisa Parida
    Metamorphosis / 131
Evie Petropoulou
    To the unknown man / 132
Claudia Piccinno
    In the alphanumeric code / 133
Jonathan Rizzo
    Children and Small Fish / 134
LaVan Robinson
    Rise / 136
Amita Sanghavi
    'Being rich' / 137
Sankha Sen
    When I met Me / 139
Tali Cohen Shabbtai
    I am Tali / 147
Robert Simon
    Friday Night in Kenesaw / 148
Anata Kumar Singh
    A Little Drop of Water / 149
Pankhuri Sinha
    The politics of re-starting / 150
Howard Stein
    In the Neighborhood / 152
Paul Stroble
    Psalm in Snow / 154
Sushant Thapa
    Bearings / 155

Jerena Tobiasen
    Best Friends / 156
    The Gardener's Mistress / 159
J R Turek
    Pillow Moon over a Night Drive / 161
Chika Udekwe
    The Flame / 162
Uche Francis Uwadinachi
    A New Beginning / 163
Amrita Valan
    The Proposal / 164
    Mercy / 166
Petros Kyriakou Veloudas
    'Moon Pocket' / 168
Julene Tripp Weaver
    The Addition of Audience: A Meditation / 170
Kari Wergeland
    Waystation / 172
John Yamrus
    i remember the last time /173
S. A. Yitta
    Beyond Whitened Skin / 175
Ewa Maria Zelenay
    A handbag / 176
Biographies / 177
Epilogue by Mutiu Olawuyi / 202

VISUALS

Photo of Robin Wyatt Dunn / 50
Every Child Matters by pj johnson Poet Laureate of the Yukon / 89
"Double Blind Placebo Affect" painting by Janet Kozachek / 95
"A White Cat Comes In" painting by Janet Kozachek / 96
"He Leads Me Beside Still Waters" taken at the Beyond Van Gogh Milwaukee Exhibit, 2021
    by Angie Mack / 103
"Artists and Brothers" taken at ArtfindZ in Hartford Wisconsin, 2021 by Angie Mack / 104
"Little Pink Anderson Visits the Grafton House of Blues with Blu"
    taken in Grafton, Wisconsin while working on Little Pink's Autobiography, 2021
    by Angie Mack / 105
Photo by Aji Ndumbeh Jobe / 116

SARFRAZ AHMED
I Remember Their Faces

People, places,
That I remember,
That I recall,
That I stumbled upon,
Some are still here,
While others are gone,

Many I could not hold onto,
No matter how hard I tried,
But many stayed here,
Long after the laughter died,

Too many strangers,
Not enough friends,
They all came into my life,
But all left in the end,

Now all I seem to do,
Is walk past gravestones,
Of those that came in my life,
Left a mark,
Did what they had to do.

Now and then I recall,
I remember,
People, places,
I remember their smiles,
And laughter,
I remember their faces.

BARTH AKPAH
Wistful smile

  I came with a bag of love
  but you hissed with a bushel of hate
  filled with adjectives? So I asked how
   do you smile and breathe in this binary
    clone of *Elegbera, esu*, the one the earth refuse to bury?

Elegbera, esu – commonly known as Yoruba god of trickster.

KEITH ALLISON
When Escape Only Leads to What You Were Running From

The headline reads,
"The Internet
Is Freaking Out
About A Dead Cow
In A Supermarket"

And, to be fair,
the cow's entrance
to the meat aisle
was astonishingly
unique

For the simple reason
that he,
unlike the endless
procession of others,
entered alive

He wasn't meant to
walk into the store
on his own,
the plans for his death
were well under way

Like so many beside him,
and countless before him,
he was packed tightly
into a truck

An involuntary passenger
with a one-way ticket
to a dismal destination:
the house of slaughter

But an overturned truck
offered the chance of escape
and off he ran
as fast as his hooves
would allow

Until the strange,
open doors
beckoned him

A respite, perhaps,
from the horror
both behind and ahead

But his supposed sanctuary
was already filled
with the bodies
of his bovine brethren,
dismantled and displayed
in coolers kept frozen
to impede their decay

A sudden bullet
sent his body to the ground,
falling lifeless
like the packaged remains
surrounding him

The customers,
it seems,
were upset that they
had so vividly
witnessed the pools
of blood seeping
from the broken remnants
of someone who,
only moments ago,
was standing
on his own four legs

They preferred
not to think
of their burgers
as dead

PAMELA ANDERSON
Gimme Back My Wig
Dedicated to: Hound Dog Taylor (1915-1975)

He's no gentleman caller, strolling up the sidewalk
to ring your bell—carrying sweet talk and a fistful of flowers.
No.
He zigzags across the lawn after midnight—
guitar slung low and fedora cock-eyed and insolent.
You know he's a tough hound to keep on the porch—
and any man who takes a straight razor to his extra finger
is flat-out crazy—but when he sings *Honey!*—
Gimme BACK my wig! you laugh all the way down to your toes.
You shimmy out from behind the screen door
and leap over the stoop onto dew-slick grass.
Take a slug from his flask—whiskey—and a dangerous draw
from his Pall Mall. You know—deep in your bones—
that you should never follow this junk-yard dog,
but it's impossible to resist his boogie-woogie beat
stomping all over your blues-loving soul.

MADELINE ARTENBERG
Apostle

Bless me Mother for you are gone
and I still sin in the hallowed halls of cinema;
nay, I am wiped clean after each showing.
Like an apostle, I followed you, mother,
followed you, queen of the double feature,
followed you into forgetting
myself, you, hard edges.

You taught me to bless the moving image,
sweet and tart fruits doled out
in two-hour portions;
you taught me to slip into other skins
as easily as we slipped into disappearing.

There was no need for the talk between us—
the cinema sirens showed me their game:
Natalie, Doris, Elizabeth,
Marilyn, bad girls and good,
seduced by rock-hard jaws.

There was no need for your seesaw rules—
I learned the commandments from jewel thieves,
double agents, pregnant nuns;
rule number one—never get caught.

When the show was over,
we'd walk the two miles home,
pink slowly fading from your flushed face,
puffy mouth and eyes receding into rigid lines;
your love for cinema tucked back inside
that place I could never find.

When the show was over,
I returned to wanting
what you could not reach,
returned to waiting,
waiting to live,
to sin,
to be cleansed
in the hallowed cinema
of beginnings, middles, ends.

previously published in *erbacce*, 2005, and in *The ANYDSWPE Anthology*, 2017.

JAN BALL
Vestments

He regularly wears patterned satins
and hand-embroidered albs to say
morning Mass. They shimmer
in the altar lights like a silver fish
in the sun. Once he entones
Go in peace, he walks to the vestry
and changes to his stiffly starched collar
and somber cassock subdued as the black
the rest of us wear: aspirants, postulants,
novices and professed sisters who all
remain kneeling until he leaves the chapel.

This last morning, he steps through the gate
in the communion rail with its white ironed linens
trimmed in lace like a Thanksgiving tablecloth.

His heels click down the two steps
from the sanctuary onto the chapel floor
almost tap-dancing past the first few stations
of the cross on the wall,
including Jesus is Condemned to Die.

We are still adjusting
to our new postulancy routines
and have never seen anyone die,
so only briefly look up
from our meditation books when we hear
the thud of a body collapse on the autumn floor
next to our pews, and hear a guttural scream
intense as a screech owl at night.

His bowels open and evacuate an earthly stench
overwhelming memories of the dignified satin vestments
he wore to elevate the host just a few minutes ago
saying: This is my body; this is my blood.

We all thought his body was immortal.

LES BERNSTEIN
Heliotropism

I am dreaming
always dreaming
a protagonist sleepwalking
these most ordinary chapters
of thought's well-worn grooves

things will always happen
an anarchy of experience
mess and distraction
bountiful and inexhaustible
in my epic novel
no one is reading

to tell a little bit of truth
here is a non-fiction version
my story is my story
my story is just a story
my story is not true

will the sleepwalker awake
to an illuminated darkness
no foothold in the mutable past
no mindless march into ephemera

can there finally be
the silencing of language
the inner symphony
with only one sustained note
of full throated living

just simple
so simple
being
and not
so simple
being
in the soft glow
of an eternal now

Bengt Björklund

the leafless birch
will not testify in open court
to the mutation
eating at its existence
there is bad blood
lurking in the shadows

one man sold his light
just to make sure
that the darkness was his own
another spotted a wave
rolling with no tomorrow
into dereliction

war is more than guns
mines and solitary bomb men
there's no excuse for the slow
to dress in wet rags
to score power points
at the market altar

stifled walled and brewing
for the sake of more
small men induce avarice
looking the other way
when all other vail
to the coming of more void

***

a wanton in need of more than I
or any one of us going nowhere
can muster or turn into a crossroad
falls into fake buckets of concern
tidal masters of old fence in silence
life never was a matter of serenity
it was always a matter of waiting
for the nemesis of total silence
there will be no other silence
waiting for in new dawn
full of birdsong and trees humming

LIN BRUMMELS
Rosie

Octoberfest venders remind
me of dill pickles in a jar
the way Rosie used to serve
them with burgers and fries
The way she plunged her bare
hand into a gallon jar of pickles
to pull out two or three slices
for each burger plate
No one had the nerve to ask Rosie
to use a fork or rubber gloves
or even to forgo the pickles
It was a time-honored tradition
to have Rosie deliver pickles
to customers
like she had been delivered
from Korea where she met Leon
stationed there
during the Korean Conflict
A war but not a declared war
leaving some veterans disabled
some disfigured and some married
to Korean women, like Rosie
married Leon

TROY CAMPLIN
Sources

My Muses are the offspring of my memory
And God. The Greeks were right. I sing my memory.

Can poets then be ignorant? Can poets fail to love?
The poets sing the songs of God from memory.

And thus I must sing songs of love and celebrate
All life, my wife, and all the joys of memory.

My joy's the joy of one who lives in Paradise
Because my trip through Hell remains in memory.

I had the shroud around my eyes burned off
So I could see the gold of my deep memory –

The human, tribes expanding into everyone
To make a network building social memory

The mammal, touch, emotion, and the lobe-finned drives
Of ritual and property in memory

Perhaps we also touch the stars in which we're born,
And back before there's time, the naught of memory.

The terror that is there will fling you back to earth
To see creation's beauty as God's memory,

And thus I live in joy because I've seen the truth,
True virtue and deep beauty through my memory.

I hope this love of life, of God, of man, my wife
Will help keep me, Troy Camplin, in your memory.

TROY CAMPLIN
The Sunflower's Reason

The wise sunflower nods toward the sun --
Its arc is eminently rational --
As is the tastiness of its ripe seeds,
Seductive kernel in the striped hull --

How clever! It gets birds to spread its seeds
And humans to domesticate it so
The species can proliferate its gold
And have its seeds protected from the snow.

The sacrifice of seeds makes perfect sense
For all the flower has to gain. It fills
The fields in monocultures it could not
Achieve alone -- it covers well-tilled hills.

The flower's flavorful seeds fulfill all
The species needs -- the choice to coexist
With other species much more rational
Than making poisons with which to resist.

The bees will get their pollen, nectar -- man
Will get the honey and the seeds, all three
Cooperating to make mutual trade,
For nothing in this life is ever free.

TANIYA CHAKRABORTY
Act

I sleep when I'm idle not in darkness…
   Those who are sitting next to seaside
   With their hungry eyes
   And hidden expectations like them
   I'm living in showing off that I'm asleep
   Sky kept the mountain in dark
   If you are honest
  Other will be brutal to you
  Actually the opposite touch
  Brings the sleeping equality…

(TRANSLATOR- SAYANTAN CHOWDHURY)

RICK CHRISTIANSEN
In London during the War

In London during the War—
The sound of dripping syrup methodically tapping a tattoo on the shelf below,
from a can of peaches pierced by bomb shrapnel
while sitting on a London apartment shelf
during the blitz.

In our plague year—
The sound of an ICU respirator
wheezing to a stop
after the code has been called.
Time of death marked by the patient's cell phone
now unplugged and placed in the bag for her children.

This Plague year has changed us all.
Time speeding up and slowing down to the rhythms of serotonin.
Anxiety creating brilliant focused experience
like a microscope being dialed in to the cellular level.

They say that in London during the war,
people felt more alive.
The Spector of sudden death from the sky
made them love faster, drink longer, fuck harder.

In our Plague year—
We endure the Spector of slow death.
Not from the sky, but from the air.

Droplets like shrapnel piercing the lungs/slowly stealing breath away.
We only grow heavier.
Eating and watching and hiding from the miasma.

They say that in London during the War,
people died alone trapped in the wreckage of bombed buildings.

In our Plague year—
people die alone trapped in hospital beds.
Tethered to machines instead of family.
Each breath more shallow than the last, until the ragged sound stops.

They say that in London during the War,
each morning people would emerge blinking.
Wearing masks against the dust and smoke.
Marking the demise of another shop or restaurant to bomb or fire
as they navigated the minimums of life.

Picking up a prescription.
Trying to find milk or toilet paper.

Because children are still thirsty
and we must shit until we die.

Wandering for items that would fill the hole
of uncertainty and named fear.

The anonymity of masked travel.
Making the eyes do all of the work of the face.
Trying to connect through fabric and fear.

In our Plague year—
It is the same.

They say that in London during the War,
 everyone pulled together.
They had the connection of a shared enemy.

In our Plague year—
we are denied that connection.
False news and finger pointing make us misdirect our resolve
away from shared purpose.
Toward disconnecting conspiracy and suspicion.

They say that in London during the War,
Everyone became stronger.

In our Plague year—

TODD CIRILLO
My First Time

It is my first time
back in a bar
since the world shut down.
Over 394 days,
I haven't missed this many
happy hours and last calls
since I was 15.
I jump at the first opportunity
to pay someone else
top dollar
to make me a well drink
while I look around
hoping for those old inspirations…
lipstick, a flash of smile,
a moment of eye contact,
summer dress walking to or away,
brushing hair back behind the right ear,
slow moving finger
over the top of a glass,
swaying hips at the jukebox.

A bartender,
sits at a table,
six feet away,
smoking,
taking a break from trying,
trying to make back
all she lost
over the last year,
hoping people will be generous enough
to cover the months of back rent,
credit card debt
and overdue bills.

I stare at the smoke
of her cigarette
slowly rising up
from the cracked, black ashtray
towards the fat, white clouds above
leaving behind a signal
I can no longer read,
so I don't even notice
her
walking away—

christ,
it's been
a long year.

TODD CIRILLO
Kick Out the Jams Motherfucker
   --for Julie Valin

She keeps going back
to the blues.
When I want her
to be Rock N Roll,
Punk's early days,
Grunge
and Heavy Metal thunder.
I simply want her
to quit fucking around,
kick out the jams
and put her stories down
onto the page.
To get those words
out to the masses.
But she
doesn't want to be a frontwoman
swinging the microphone centerstage,
frontpage of all the magazines,
busting heads,
hearts and guitar strings.
She simply wants to hold onto
the slow rhythm
of back porch blues
with a melody
that doesn't burn out
or fade away
but drifts across the years
until eventually everyone hears it
and realizes
this is where it all began.

DAVIDE ROCCO COLACRAI
Ma-*la*-voglia

There's in the short froth of a palpitation
a God waiting like a chrysalis
creating the waves' host
on which lazes my name

summer dust on figs are words
when sunset makes them red-hot by pulp
at the sunset's forgiveness where the silence salt,
the shore burnt like skin smelling Malvasia

the scorching stones at the olives' bottom
they sigh like the heart's untamed rings,
when the fishermen offshore suspend the nostalgia of the sea
and undo the distance from who we let go
in the line of the horizon

so many stories tell the rocks,
some get caught on the nets,
other collected on the water's edge like shells,
who smells them is a wet snout of a dog
or the crying in which was dried out a dream.

My city is sleeping.

The pain washed by the seaweeds at the fan of Mistral.

I'm counting all my happinesses
on the noise's end,
while a seagull is carring love affairs in dialect,
and the sign of the cross a lucky charm.

PAT CONNORS
Burning Hunger

Andrew King has a burning hunger. It keeps him from falling asleep during the long Queen streetcar ride westward to work, and from tuning out the lady who sits beside him to tell her story.

"My daughter is a witch. Oh, oh migawsh, can you believe that's really a thing? She wear a, what you call, a pinta…penta-…"

"A pentagram," Andrew says, conjuring up images of old heavy metal videos.

"Pentagram, that's it, dear. She wear a pentagram around her neck, like gypsy. Like this, you see? She says it means nothing, but I am not stupid woman, I know better!

"Anyways, she dating this boy, nice Christian boy, named Dolinsky.

"Dolinsky! Have you ever heard a Christian boy named Dolinsky?"

"No, I haven't," Andrew admits.

"Anyways, I think this boy thinks he can change my daughter. Or maybe he have something else to hide, if you know what I mean."

"I honestly don't," Andrew shrugs.

"Oh, such a nice young man like you doesn't need to listen to…Here's my stop, anyways! Thank you putting up the ramblings of a lonely woman. I sure hope you not a writer. Have a nice day, now!"

"Thank you very much. You too."

Andrew shakes his head, almost unsure if the conversation really happened, or if he perhaps imagined it during his typical morning reverie.

He hopes it did happen, because he does like to listen. It keeps him from feeling like he is self-absorbed, pre-occupied with his burning hunger.

*

His burning hunger gets him through the morning greetings and other rituals, and the desire to turn them into a Monty Python skit. It gets him through his constitutional in the bathroom he fears may be rife with some malady. It keeps his hand from shaking too much as he gets his first coffee. It gets him through the clotted cream – not English style, merely left out too long the previous day – and the open sugar jar, granules clumped and dotted a dull brown.

It gets him through the tired one-one-one with the even more tired assistant manager, who has been having the same day for many years. It gets him through his first contact with the internal customer who grunts and groans and moans through a bad hangover, then ends the conversation proclaiming, "What a night I had last night!" It gets him through the second contact with the external customer who wants to know why things didn't go right the first time.

It almost gets Andrew through his glimpse of her for whom his heart aches and has always ached in some ancient way which will never end: he goes over to talk to her, and now knows what was meant by whomever coined the curious phrase, 'My heart was in my mouth.'

"G… mornin', Gloria."

"Good Morning, Andrew. You look nice today. How are you?"

Suddenly, he doesn't know, but manages to say, "Um, fine," and, "Have a nice day," before going back to the break room to regroup.

He takes a deep breath, realizes who he is, reminded of his burning hunger.

*

It gets Andrew through the drudgery of his work, which doesn't challenge him, doesn't force him to use his abilities, doesn't appeal to his passion, which he accepts because it more than pays the bills, and that is, after all, what grown-ups do.

His burning hunger gets him through to lunchtime. Oh, how he loves to eat! Sweet, sour, salty, spicy, it's all good to him. No food is too exotic for Andrew.

Today, though, it's comfort food at a diner with his old friend Jeff, a courier who meets him on his rounds.

"Married life isn't all it's cracked up to be, Andrew. I mean, Shelley is great, and I love the girls, but it's a great big hassle, you know what I mean?"

"Why is it impossible in the 21st century to get a club sandwich with mayonnaise already on it?"

"Are you even listening to me?"

"Marriage is a great big hassle," Andrew paraphrases with frustration, as well as the underlying hope he will experience such difficulty himself.

From there he smiles and nods a lot, gets mayonnaise for his sandwich, gravy for his French fries, and another glass of iced tea. Andrew loves Jeff almost like a brother, but it seems like they have this conversation every time they meet.

Sometimes it gets hard not to be cynical, to not anticipate the appropriate time to say, "Things will be different when…"

But Andrew likes Jeff's company, and it keeps his mind off his burning hunger.

*

It gets him through the afternoon, the involuntary food coma, the inevitable confrontation with the bafflingly embittered co-worker, the insufferable afternoon meeting, which would be so much easier to fake interest in with the aid of fresh morning coffee.

Then, almost at the end of the work day, core duties done; a collective sigh of relief. Everyone shares their after-work itinerary, which somehow melds into one. "I've got to take Jimmy to soccer practice. I've got a date with Gus. Tammy has her dance recital. Poor Bobbie (or is it Bobby) has to go to the Doctor with rickets."

…Jimmy has taken to dance with the Doctor…Gus has a date with Tammy…Bobbie and Bobby at the Robbie for soccer…I've got to go to the ricket recital…or, words to that effect, which seem to have no effect…yet do…

Truth be told, sometimes – well, most days – Andrew longs for such mundanities and the order of the routine they would provide; the proof of apparent normalcy. But not today.

Today, it's off to The Rex for hockey talk with the two co-workers he gets along with this week. Hockey is the great ice-breaker between men - with the right sort it can be the whole conversation. Plus, it keeps him from wondering what they might be saying about him to anyone else.

"What the Leafs need," the oldest one says with a sense of authority, "is a power forward with some upside."

"What they need," says the younger one, eager to prove himself right, "is a number one defenseman not on the downside."

Andrew has waited as long as he could, but now it is time to say his piece. "What they need is, a goalie who can make a save in the shootout." Then, to make sure the argument was won, "Three more beers and three shots please!"

"Yessir."

"You are the man, Andrew!"

"You are the king," an unfortunate play on words which nearly halted the banter.

"Actually, I prefer to think of myself as a king among men," was Andrew's retort, met by garrulous yet mirthless laughter.

It is so much easier, though much less meaningful, when the names of "the boys" change every week. No expectations, no promises of future fealty or companionship required, no one has to remember anyone's birthday.

Everyone can be themselves, as long as they are not truly themselves. A composite of the perception of who the other two might really be, the image of the guy at the office you all want to be, your funny younger brother, and the hero of your former high school's football team. You can have the best hours of your week like this, and you can reliably have them every week. You can even almost let your guard down.

Until it is time to go back to the burning hunger.

*

Andrew leaves The Rex when the band comes on, his burning hunger numbed if not sated by the alcohol and the company. He would have liked to listen to some jazz, just to hear something different, but he knew if he stayed at the bar for another hour or two, he would never make it to work the next morning.

He realizes he forgot to go to the washroom before leaving as soon as he steps into an icy puddle. However, he wants to make sure he gets the eastbound streetcar for the long ride home, and knows he would never catch the next one if he went back inside.

The streetcar is packed, although past rush hour, and Andrew stands in a crowd of excited couples, their evening just begun. At University, many get off, bumping Andrew's elbow or kicking his leg without apology. They are replaced by young families going home from who knows where, although apparently the same place. These are louder and more excited and even less concerned about Andrew's personal space than the previous crowd.

Andrew feels, even thinks, these people have planned to make him miserable, or at least remind him of his loneliness, a sadness which turns his burning hunger into even more inaction, more self-pity.

By Yonge Street the car is half empty, so Andrew sits down, leans his head against the window. Through Riverdale, through Leslieville, he looks at everyone and everything which passes by, but sees nothing. He dozes off near Coxwell, for a few moments of the peace he rarely experiences during the night.

He sees and is part of a light so bright, so warm, he feels nurtured and loved, forgets his selfish self-hating bitterness, embraces the unknown blessings which are to come.

"Next stop, Neville Park Boulevard," announces the falsely soothing automated voice.

"Last stop, sunshine," admonishes the street car driver. "Wakey-wakey."

"S-sorry," Andrew gets himself together.

"Are you okay, buddy?"

"Well, I'm home."

LORRAINE CURRELLEY
We've Done This Before

I don't want nor need studies and calls for gatherings filled with the stench
of murderers bullets and discussions on racial conciliation.
We've done this before, before, and before.
I don't want nor need Black and pale hand holders socializing death while
singing we shall overcome.
We've done this before, before, and before.
I don't want nor need momentary sorrow. I inherited my own sorrow, pain
and trauma at my birth and live with it still.
I don't want nor need secreted back room meetings and deals protecting
entitlement and privilege, while pale silence and inaction sanctions my
death.

I do want and need unburied sons and daughters of Black mothers and fathers to rise, Not on the third
day but now!
I do want and need Black mothers and fathers to awaken freed from raped dreams of pale terror to
find their nine months safe.
I do want and need Blacks to speak in truth and end the going along to get along madness. Cowering
Blacks never wanting to be those angry Black men and women. Never wanting to offend the
sensibilities of those unworthy of our collective Black humanity.

I do want Whites to disrupt their families, friends, communities and selves,
damning the murders of Black men, women and children.
I do want injustice to dismount her whorishness and open both her eyes like she does her legs.

KATE CUMISKEY
Cokeheads I have known

Apparently I know lots of cokeheads. I've figured this out by my husband saying *well he's a cokehead,* lots of times. About different people. Once I started thinking about it I realized maybe I like them. Maybe it's the energy, or the money, two things I've never had. You want what isn't part of you, right? Next to these

people I'm in a coma. Maybe it's a lethargy deep within my DNA I can't shake. The contrast is envy-inducing. Try as I might, money's never mattered a whit & if you do coke apparently it has to. *Cokeheads don't tend to share;* another tidbit from Mikel, *it's not like pot.* Mikel and I smoked a lot: in fact, hash brought us

together, back on the 24-hour drive-on beach. In my parents' blue Chevy station wagon. I have a good understanding of marijuana, then and now; follow the politics. But cocaine eludes me so I miss it in others. I lost a friend—which always feels like failure but in this case is a good thing—over not letting her manage me. She

said things like, I'll pick you up at two. We always dress up for the mall, no jeans, and, Don't you realize you're too political? That last comment only got fifteen likes on Facebook. I looked at the river under the moon, passed the joint back and replied, *What you don't understand is I like myself. The way I dress, how*

I look; my work, my family. I'm happy with who I am. That tore it. We were done. Even though these days she's a Trumper, it feels like failure. Still. Several business owners I admire around town apparently have coke problems. Or coke solutions. Hard for me to judge, I refuse to, because I have fucked up more ways than you

could count. Cashed in my retirement to go visit my brother in Hawai'i because Mother asked me to. She felt bad nobody had, so I grabbed the money, took three of our four sons, stayed a month. The thing he remembers, the story he tells, is how I borrowed $900 to get home. These choices, being a teacher and having four kids,

marrying a fireman, choosing k-12 instead of higher ed., grad degrees, who's to say that's not worse than a cocaine habit? Not giving a shit about money, sinking your heart in a place that is disappearing under a warm salt sea, what's worse? The first meth head I really got to know made a cripplingly generous parenting

decision I had to watch, giving her daughter up because of love. Something sober me could never do, no matter what. Who's to judge the cokeheads? Me? You? What's your flaw? Have you ever asked yourself that, passing by the guy with a cardboard sign on the off ramp to I-95?

BILL CUSHING
Music

"Music isn't about standing still and being safe."
— Miles Davis (1926 - 1991)

listen

two weeks after you died
a quarter-million thronged
by the St. Johns River
to hear the music you had spawned
hoping to see you
but
even in death
you never looked back

they were all there
    Hannibal   Bird
    Chick   Jo-Jo
    Red   Jaco
    Bean   Dizzy
    my favorite Freddie Freeloader

isolated
you
were a beacon
    a flagship for messages
        of the heart

back to the crowd unbowed
that proud dance-walk
announced by muted horn
that spoke
and broke
through all the bull
and told us about a place

Miles

ahead of everyone else
you spent a lifetime
    thinking for yourself
    speaking to every generation
playing it all:
    jazz   blues
    funk   rock

  fusion
categories took
a backseat
to creativity
  and rhythm

  space

  and feeling
   spirit

I remember fourth grade
picking up a horn
then laying it down
rock and roll was my world
what did I know

seven years later I heard

it was in the Garden
where you brought me back
to music

I walked all the way home

Miles

from that train station
my head pounding with sounds
frantic-fast as the subway
I spent the night on
  those African rhythms
  you used decades
  before anyone else
  even thought to
filling my head
letting me know
I'd have it all down cold
if I could walk
as cool as the notes you heard
  coming from

Miles

you had that thing
  that style
that spark that was

a blue flame
    jumping
    off a gas stove
igniting everything everywhere
touching the genetic
resonant
frequency
in all

First published in *Stories of Music*, vol 1; part of the collection *A Former Life*

MAHUA DAS
Colour

The colour of each relationship is different from another.
Some are deep red like emarald,
Some are light blue like dream,
Some are sweet pink like tulip,
Some are like the laughter of yellow rose.
When one relationship starts,
it's colour is light green like new paddy field or the leaves of baby plantain.
Or then, it's like baby grasses.
Slowly, the colour of life becomes darker,
One day the colour matures.
In the meantime, storm, typhoon, rain ,thunder everything comes in life.
We all are compelled to tackle all the disasters.
We cannot realise when the colour of life grows into grey.
Then we turn into the black and white movie.

MILI DAS
When I will go to the stars

When I am no more in the world
You must remember, I am missing the world.
I never want to leave the earth,
But it is the last destiny of our life.
Don't fell any tears in front my body.
I am not habituated to see your mournful face.

When you would go away from me
You never forget to hold my hand
And kiss my palm.
Don't be afraid of cold touch.
Remember I will wait there for you.

How only man can leave the earth?
Sun moon and stars moves on millions of years in the same way.
Why human beings can't?

When I am no more in the world,
you will be free.
Have you ever seen -
Man can comeback again !
Why lament for me.
Now you are free and I am also free.
I have never come for quarrel with you.
Never tell you please love me once more.
I am arriving at eternal living
Good bye my love.

NANDITA DE NEE CHATTERJEE
When children cry themselves to sleep…

Have you seen the fear
In her eyes?
She's afraid to rise
Afraid to cast her cloak of darkness on the world
When she alone strides the skies
Awake
Watchful

Daunted, the Moon eclipses her light
Ashamed
A celestial being
Privy to the dark shadows on earth
Wakeful
Shutting her ears to the cries
Rising every night from the earth

Little children wailing
Mothers shedding silent tears
Prayers to no avail
Children going hungry at night

Where children go to sleep hungry
A kaleidoscope of lights glitter all night
Where crying babies
Are silenced by blaring horns
Where children toss and turn
The world rests blissfully unconcerned

Where pangs of hunger
Are perennial nightmares
Where dreams of full plates
Haunt hundreds still
Where apples and oranges
Never hang free on roadsides
Where have-nots have seen it all

The pains
The suffocation
Unchanging destinies
Roofless
Jobless
Hopeless…

The abysmal images
Of the wretched
Reach high into the skies
She hides her face in shame
Throwing dark clouds on the disgrace

For a world that is culpable
A crying shame on humanity
Thriving with apathy
When children cry themselves to sleep

When children cry themselves to sleep.

NANCY AVERY DAFOE
Three-page excerpt from Memoir: *Unstuck in Time, A Memoir and Mystery on Loss and Love*

One: In All These Other Moments, Blaise is Fine

I had three children, and then, there are two. Searching desperately, I find a photo. There is a crease near the edge where it was accidently bent. Here is a picture of my son Blaise Martin at four. I'm kneeling beside him on the wide dock attached to our sloping lawn with other end hanging precariously over shallow water. One of the supporting legs of the dock is tilted. Blaise as a little boy, in this photograph, looks skeptical, likely about the possibility of catching a fish, but I'm certain he will, my younger self all smiles and anticipation for the day, his future, because I cannot imagine an unfolding of life in which my son does not exist.

Deep breath. Looking everywhere for photographs of Blaise, digging through old albums and a drawer filled with loose pictures, I experience rising alarm. "We don't have enough photos of him," I yell, feeling helpless.

"What are you talking about, Mom? There are pictures of Blaise in every room," my daughter Nicole said, trying to calm me in the days following my son's death at the age of thirty-two.

My lovely second child was right, of course, but what she did not acknowledge in the moment was why I was so frantic: there would never be enough photos of Blaise again. I needed to see him everywhere because I could not see him anywhere. Having to rely on my memory alone for my son caused such angst that I had to stop and sit to catch my breath every few minutes.

"The real person is so very different from our imaginings, from our flawed memories that pick and choose the frame," wrote great British writer C.S. Lewis in his memoir *A Grief Observed* about the loss of his wife Helen Joy Gresham. Lewis, too, was unsatisfied with memories as his only link to his beloved.

What would happen when my own imperfect imagination could not readily bring forth images of Blaise's face exactly, his voice, his gestures, his words? Physical manifestation of emotional havoc is the reality I experienced after the death of my son.

I had accepted beauty and terror, as Rilke suggested, locking out no emotion as difficult as that can be. If I am to be repeatedly menaced by repetitions of the scene of my son's death, I have also remained cognizant of the beauty of his life, beauty he brought to me in daily acts, athletically graceful movements, kindness to people he knew whom I did not know at the time but am now welcoming. Of course, death is final, and yet, death cannot take every memory, our will to recall. Blaise is just "unstuck in time," as Kurt Vonnegut wrote about Billy Pilgrim in his novel *Slaughterhouse-Five*.

I, too, came unstuck in time but with less positive connotations, as in unglued, come apart, rattled, floored. Forward motion seemed impossible for a time, not simply difficult after my son died. Even when I was physically moving, I had no recollection of having gotten from one place to another. I made myself consider other parallels to the strings of time that could loop back upon themselves. I followed my senses to the stories of my son's life.

We wake daily to an assault of information, pictures of violence from tragedies of the world constantly coming at us through our media. If we are decent human beings, we are aware and empathic to others' sorrows and great misfortunes. On some level, however, we delude ourselves into believing this or that calamity will not happen to us. Then, tragedy strikes directly into our busy lives. In the face of great loss, what we previously thought of as catastrophe is suddenly less than. We cannot insulate ourselves. Moment to moment, we are caught in tornados of emotion and memory.

Opening an album, I am struck by a black and white photograph someone took of Blaise as a baby. Here in a scrapbook is a card from Dr. Wang, wishing his patients a Merry Christmas. In this photo, Dr.

Wang is a young man. My children's pediatrician measured my toddler and remarked that he thought Blaise would be 6'5" when he was grown. How kindly, perceptive Dr. Wang so accurately predicted my son's adult height is uncanny. How he later missed early signs of Marfan syndrome is completely understandable but, on another level, unforgivable.

Closing one photo album, I open another. A photo of my son at five. His smile is feint as if he is trying to produce the desired effect because his mom asked, but the day is not quite what he had hoped. His little brows are knitted, and his eyes glance to the right as if there is something out of camera range that is causing concern. But he appears the picture of health. Maybe he just did not want his picture taken again. Perhaps the shadow across his face is not worry but something else entirely, another mistake of interpretation. Knowledge of his sudden death at thirty-two impinges on every photograph of him now. This is not foreshadowing, I tell myself.

During the last month of his life, I retained that small cadre of new messages from my son. I look at those texts now and think, he had fourteen days left to live. On that date, he had ten days left to live. He had four days left of his life. His tragic death elevated those trivial notes to ones of gravity, of consequence and ridiculous value.

Mystery of our temporality, and the question of how to mark "we were here," remain. This import is why we suffer over wording on gravestones, fantasize about our legacies. Blaise moved through the world quietly, dynamically, and with uncommon grace in every sense of the word, and at the end, showing extraordinary kindness to others. I can only give him my meager words.

Struggling over what to have incised on his gravestone, we came to accept his sister Nicole's suggestion for her brother because each phrase rang true to the boy and the man.

Ever Cool
Ever Kind
Ever Thoughtful
Ever Young.

ZLATAN DEMIROVIC
Your Eyes in Glass of Sorrow

Your eyes in glass of sorrow
rosemary scent and picture on the lap

Memories full of roses
And dreams of guilt with pain
Childish, bittersweet refrain
This little soldier in the left brain
Singing songs of sadness
Fighting to sustain

Your eyes in glass of sorrow
rosemary scent and picture on the lap

Heavy rains with clouds of dust
vanishing the stories on pictorial scene
melting everlasting blue reflection on the screen

There was a boy in flame of passion
it burned him to the skin and bone
Once he was awakened by the scream of love
reminded that his true love's gone

Don't ever challenge a vulnerable child
his wounds are deep enough
he bears the heart of the bravest soldier

Never ever say to someone "you old man"
Don't ever disregard the wrinkles of wisdom
Carousel of life is shining in a bigger picture
The wheel of blindness, turning up and down…

He's sitting calm now,
observing the sky,
breathing the stardust…

Your eyes in glass of sorrow
rosemary scent and picture on the lap…

LINDA TROTT DICKMAN
Star of the Sea
For Emily Rachael

At the heart of Italy, in the City of Castles
a warm song was born
Embodied in Marietta Alboni
her very name meaning *Star of the Sea*.

Rossini favored her, trained her
toured this rare voice-among-women,
the deepest known.

Whitman, in love with Italian opera
fell deeply into the inviting waters
of her voice, vibrato, venerable
Queen among contraltos.

The depths reached his very essence.
The heights wreathed him in light.
Her swirling notes,
spanning the length of a single word
lifted him
Giving naisance to a song of his own.

CASEY DORMAN
U-Dub,* 1965

We had such hope then, or at least I did
Leaving the library, barefoot along the Ave
Taking Sartre seriously and nothing for granted

Cherry blossoms populated the Quad
Dead Roethke sang from the wood
While Dylan sang through his nose

Rage in the streets and love in the parks
Angels in rags and satyrs with Afros
Cymbals and drums and garlanded babies

Bergson and Marcel, Husserl and Heidegger
Beckett and Pinter, Camus and Genet
Coffee and cigarettes, hashish and beer

A world paused in its gyre, we all held our breath
A moment suspended, poised in becoming
Certain that we would determine the outcome

The day after yesterday drawing to end
Slogans still echo inside of my head
When will the dreams stop and what happens then?

*U-Dub is a nickname for the University of Washington in Seattle

SHERRI FELT DRATFIELD
Millie Collins, Your Barn Is Gone

Obbie cleared it after folks
on our road said outright
kids would get hurt.
The floor'd been mostly missing
since just before you died
and took your DAR roots to the grave,
not to mention that poor
nameless mongrel you kept staked
in the front yard.
Never saw him fed or taken in.
Never told you I tossed him bones from the car.

Ob's a fixer but once the roof sagged
that barn was done.
He and Brenda bought your place
from the gal who'd taken care of you
(can't think her name)
those last years. Only good thing
may be you ever did, Millie,
leaving your place to that good woman.

This week, Obbie put a big red barn
just where yours was. Just where.
I watched the whole time Ob was at it. Odd
to see newness on the spot
where, so long ago, you and I
went late one night,
after drinking your cheap tea from chipped cups,
and dug that tiny grave,
deep enough.

This is the Title Poem of Dratfield's recent poetry collection, Millie Collins, Your Barn Is Gone, published in 2021 by Cervena Barva Press.

ROSE DREW
ReFocus

He must love taking tests,
mind blank except for facts;
numbers instead of memories, now
exiled behind problems he can solve.

Someone has dropped their end of the piano -
all those expectations -
the entire family resting on the lid,
waiting aside the wilting blooms.

The kids who live: Is it any wonder
their knees buckle,
their will frays,
when so much depends on them.

I bet he's grateful for assessments. Scores 100 every time.
Facts are not subjective,
do not demand,
not in dispute;

he is not left to mourn missed clues.

ROBIN WYATT DUNN
Grace can not be limited

Grace can not be limited; though its dimensions of necessity slip back beneath the eyelids to disguise its reaches, both in dream and waking life, extending back beyond the reach of your vision, though not so far back—just far enough to slip from sight.

There are engines who drive over the night, when I was a boy—and even now—the dark highways listen for the sound of the dew. And the balloons rise over the infinite field of the plain, where they have planned to arrive.

Trees set against morning mist:

Birds nestle wise against the stems and clumps of grass.

We can all say what it is: like a canoe, the minutes of morning, the certain viscosity of the air, the friendliness of birds from a particular distance, and the invitation of the sky:

Set back against the mind for its vista. The years a kind of couch.

Is it death to know the earth? In these visitations—years pressed back and forth between the body so that time itself does not exist, except as eternity.

I am coming into the balloon, and the engine is revving up, and the cigarette smoke presses against the glass, and the birds rest back against the morning, fed for now—the sky does not see us yet and we can only barely see it—

Pressed against the grass. What is it? Grace could only be a kind of rest, or the right instant of photography—or its inverse, before any photographs are taken, and yet the nature of photography is implicit in our stance against the grass, to lift in to our hands the sounds of the earth, pressed against the morning.

Perhaps I am a bird too—not yet able to fly. Trying to remember where I put my flyers, in my backpack, under the bed. In the trunk in my mother's garage, forgotten, almost entirely—

Who is it coming over the grass, awakened by the sound of the dawn, balloons rising, the ballooners parking in the field to flame their jets and lay out their fabrics, and the dark spaces of the continent shifting again to light reveal our cousins in the trees, curious to see what sort of mischief we will undertake—

Before they are ready. Or after they have already passed, overhead:

I'm flying.

Photo of Robin Wyatt Dunn

ALEX R. ENCOMIENDA
Sexageddon

At Club Bonneville, 12:30am

Sheridan walked up to the bar after carefully eying the scene. There were women in groups, men who were jumping up and down in toxic ecstasy at the center of the floor and more people dressed in provocative clothes. The sex culture was blazing fiery and rapidly amongst the young people and not everyone was going home a lucky guy.

"Let me get a shot of whiskey and a can of red bull," said Sheridan.

As he was waiting for his drinks, he saw a woman who looked vulnerable. In *his* mind, she was perfect. She looked attractive enough to have sex with and yet carried this aura of insecurity. It was almost as if she would be generally unnatractive to most men but he knew that he had a fondness for those kinds of women.

He had done this several times before. He picked someone up and went home as a lucky guy. He thought, if anything, he can at least get a taste of what she's like.

"Hi, I'm Sheridan. Is this seat taken?" he asked.

"No, go ahead."

"I see a fine woman sitting by herself and I *have* to ask, are you single? By the way, what is your name?"

She smiled. "I'm single but I'm quite happy that way. I know most of these men are looking for someone to hook up with but I'm not that kind of girl. And the name is Ella."

"Well, perhaps we can just talk and get to know each other, Ella. I can assure you, I'd be worth your while. If we end up liking each other, perhaps, we can make out. No harm in that, right?"

"I just told you, I don't do that stuff. I'm here to have a good time. I've never put out before traditionally dating someone and I won't start now. I only have sex with someone I'm in a serious relationship with. I'm not like those other women. If that's what you're after, find someone else," she replied.

The bartender gave Sheridan his drinks. He took the shot of whiskey and then chased it with the red bull.

"Oh yeah, that was good," he exclaimed.

He caught her looking at him.

"How can you drink whiskey like that? It's disgusting."

"You'd be surprised. As a matter of fact, human beings are a great species. Did you know that theoretically, a human can consume twenty ounces of vodka and not be drunk in the slightest? It's all a matter of how you drink it. Same goes with sex. Did you know that a woman can have an orgasm so strong, she can trick the physiological reaction into a constant surge of prolactin which will make her orgasm for several hours straight? Yeah, just when you might have thought you got the raw end of Darwin's deal, God throws you a puzzle box."

"That's bullshit," she replied.

"Well, believe it or not, it happens. Wanna find out for yourself?"

She smiled. "Does this kind of talk usually get you laid?"

"Not gonna lie, It's helped me before."

She paused. He noticed a glare in her eyes that wasn't there before.

"What are you, like a scientist or something?"

"Well, I'm more of a philosopher but I don't believe in pseudo-intelligence. And don't get me started on COD philosophy either. I simply take things from life that make sense to me and use them as a tool to shape myself. All of life is much more complex than we give it credit for."

She nodded her head. "Well, that's awesome. I really hope you find what you're looking for."

Sheridan bit his lip. "Do you want to go to a park or something? Perhaps, take a walk. It's getting kind of stifling here."

She gave him a blank stare and then replied, "Okay."

At Miranda Gentry Park, 2:15am

Sheridan rested his head back with his left arm against the wheel. Ella was sitting shotgun. Both were observing the train station across the street. They watched the trains pass by as he continued to elaborate on the philosophy of sex. The concept of the 80/20 rule came up and he went on about eugenics and the art of being a *Chadlite*.

"Do you know what you need in your life, Ella. You need someone who won't bullshit you and knows what he wants right away. You need the raw, closeness of being passionate and intimate with someone for the sake of your own mortality."

He slowly reached over and put his hand on her thigh. "Kiss me. We don't have to do anything else, Ella. I can trust that we'll both go home lucky if we share this one kiss."

She raised her head and he saw her eyes glistening from the reflection of the street lights. He knew that although he didn't get to have her completely, he was satisfied with just the taste of her lips and to feel them push against his.

He can go home with that. If not for the instant, carnal gratification, then for his ego and self esteem.

As he was glaring deeply into her eyes, he saw her reach below her waist. She hurried to pull up her red checkered skirt and removed her underwear. "I want it, Sheridan. Give it to me. Pound me, Sheridan!"

Although, and rightfully so, in a state of awe and disbelief, Sheridan proceeded to remove his garments and eagerly lifted up the middle armrest so that he could lay her down and get on top of her. He felt her warm, bare skin against his chest and smelled her warm, sweet breath fill his nostrils. However, something was wrong. He touched himself and he realized that he was limp. He did not understand his lack of physical sexual response as he was clearly aroused.

Confusion.

"Is something wrong?" she asked.

In a state of panic and humiliation, desperate to say anything, he uttered, "I- I'm sorry, I don't know what happened. I'm just nervous, that's all. Did you want to give me your number and we can do this another night?"

Ella hurried to put her clothes back on and abruptly left his car, slamming the door behind her.

There was quietness and then the blaring horn of an incoming train from afar.

DEIRDRE FAGAN
Dish by Dish

Today, I filled the sink with soapy water and carefully removed
all the china from the mahogany cabinet, dish by dish.

Sun reflected in the glass during my final push of the darkened door,
grandmother's egg coddler and the pinecones from your uncle's
grave shifting among the urned ashes, as I wiped my hands
on my worn apron, pondering what sits in any cabinet.

Sometimes, it's all too much.

Scalding my hands, I gently sponged and dried each, then
brusquely stacked them on the everyday shelf above the banana
tree, toaster, and breadcrumbs, among the canning-jar drinking
glasses, and father's cheap floral plates nostalgically glued back together.

Tonight, and every night, we will dine off the Haviland,
occasionally breaking one, or with some hope, two with daily life.
We will will the letting go with laughter, with crashing joy, and
without wincing.

After it all, what are we waiting for?
Or is it, *whom*?

PEG FOX
The Night Light

They looked up from the beginning of their time on Earth,
   held captive by the luminosity in the night time sky.
As men, women and children, they wondered,
   who made these lights in the sky?
Perhaps some energy or magic tried to talk, the way they talked
   when painting bison, horses, or bears in caves.
They looked up from the beginning of their time on Earth. Astonished -
   night time lights appeared, disappeared and reappeared.
The light Einstein would bend, and Planck would call quantum,
   light appearing everywhere.
A mysterious light hidden in the men, women and children,
   who wondered, and found comfort in knowing
That they did not know. They went on wondering
 why and how and from where this light shone.
A compass that gave them direction
   at night and discovery by day.

DAMON FREED
On Thinking and Feeling in Our Work of the World's in Today's Worlds

It could just be me, but it would seem if you were writing prose these days – we either come to them through one or the other, Jack Kerouac or Charles Bukowski – as a man writing prose, anyways.

The realest by way of the written word through dialogue was Bukowski in more recent years. He pushed the envelopes of bastards, junkies, both lowbrow and high, mostly; both broken and honored. His work is slightly conventional in hindsight though, adhering mainly to the one and two punches throughout, and an uppercut knockout in the ends – tying his dialogues together on one hand, and leaving us hanging on the other, to contemplate the work. Kerouac's narratives are surreal at points, telling the same kind of stories with improvisational characters in a subtler inventive prosody.

His, ebbing and flowing, through chaotic activity oriented around love stories, captured the culture in rawistic provocative ways. There is a deeper energy to his loving stories, which are imbued with abstraction through unknowingly and progressive tangents. Surprising transitions of thinking that work lovingly, along our ways to the ends of his poems of felt expression and of thought.

Bukowski is a symbol of uncompromising structure in his work, whereas Kerouac is a symbol of organic romance of thought in his work, but not in his life. People give gripes to both, Bukowski, the idiot in his work! Kerouac the goody two-shoes upper classman of thought in his work. I'd say each's work is necessary to describe our culture in today's world getting through to each through our poems is necessary as is our own work of today's times which is needed to adhere lovingly to our own progressive feeling.

Poetry wise, it seems to me to be a vaster gamut of feeling, in our poems! From total and expanding abstractions, to cohesive and formal, preaching even, poems of thoughtfulness. In this mess of what to do about it, we range from the political to love poems. From tragedy to comedy! And in paintings, it's similar.

We are fraught with what to do the same. But not in the same ways! In visual art there is realism (the depiction of lifelike things.), abstraction (the combining tactics of realism and nonobjectivism), and the nonobjective (no real-life objects depicted in paintings.) This is what we do as artists in today's world! Me, most exclusively touches on each! Yet, we understand nonobjectivism to be the most compelling mode of abstraction. So if you want to be on the edge, I recommend selling your souls. To adhere mainly, to life through art and poetry.

CINDY FRENKEL
Slumber and Awakening

Blue eyes searching, lips latching on,
she wouldn't let go of me until sleep took hold.
Now, nearly grown and hazel-eyed, she studies Latin
in the other room, eats pasta that she's rolled.
She alternates between two beds, two homes,
with the constancy of female friends.

Waving her hands as if conducting the wind,
she talks of boys, first-shaven. Invisible, I drive.
Girls in the back seat, their voices still high and sweetly soft,
overlay each other's phrases in counterpoint.
There must have been a goddess I've never read about
who gathers stars only to disperse them.
She opens her palms and stars spill out,
enough to occupy the universe.
The road ahead's so bright it almost hurts.

appeared in my chapbook The Plague of the Tender-Hearted and was first published in Peninsula Poets, where it won First Place in the Family Category from Michigan Poetry Society.

#MADMUSINGS
Boorish Bonhomie!

Bind them, keep them chained!
Squash their thinking, lock their brains!
Least you supply them knowledge any
They would then demand their rights many!
How would you rule them then?
They would comprehend your evil games!
Of how you fool them, keep them deprived,
How they hopelessly struggle to survive!
Mutilate their intellect, maul their existence
Strategically curb all resistance!
Aware they would revolt against you,
Any facility extended, you shall rue!
Slaves they are, you are the neo age king,
They must in their slogans, your praises sing!
You are the monarch of today!
Bow down to you they must anyway!
To swindle you need to cultivate fools
An intelligent mind would question your rule.
How then shall corruption flourish and bloom?
Only a handful rejoice, rest decay in gloom!
Consciously you must cultivate filth and squalor,
How else you may flaunt your dollars?
Your loathsome loot would be caught,
You shall then in prison rot!
Delude the poor with your glib
Each dreams of theirs meticulously nip!
Beguile them, keep them as living dead,
Unaware, illiterate, they would be afraid!
They shall follow and obey you like a dog,
Worship you like living God!
Never let education be showered on them,
Keep them impoverished, their minds locked and chained!

SHASWATA GANGOPADHYAY
About Dwarfs

Dwarfs are a special species of bonsai plant, who
Can move their limbs and walk at their sweet will.
They are by nature morose, those few here and there
Who have learnt to laugh, join in the circus as jokers
The rest of them wearing and raising high heels of 4 inches
Try to grab within their fists the sun that leans
From the horizon in the light of sadness of last afternoon
Later they put the sun into their mouths like round -shaped lozenge

As along the trunks of trees, the annual orbit
Remains in the rings within rings
So also in the balls of the limbs of a dwarf
Their age lurks in muscles
They cannot make friendship with giraffes,
Even ants avoid their company
Only from the reverse side of the earth
A few girls of almost near height along the equator
Come to them after constant search

But how and when to understand that
They are actually not men but trees?
When at the time of shaving in the morning, just out of haste
There's a cut on the cheek by blade
It's not blood, but sticky gum
Coming in drops from the inside of the deep skin
It's like using an axe upon the bodies of trees

DAVIDSON GARRETT
Blasted Out of Dixie

My final farewell conjures darkness,
passionate teardrops of freezing rain
fall from a sky sobbing golf-ball hail
surprising the slumbering New South,
blanketing weary magnolias with snow,
turning its fertile land into thick ice.

A twelve-hundred-mile escape on ice
ahead, my car flees in winter darkness
a town buried under glacial snowdrifts—
more accustomed to gentle spring rain
and lyrical breezes singing southerly,
than for precision bombing by hard hail.

The perilous odyssey brings *Hail
Marys* to the lips—as the blue auto Ice
Capades on the slippery highway, south
of the river that evokes gothic darkness—
while the white night vies for a regal reign,
battling the moonlight with clouded snow.

Vicksburg surrenders to the Snow
Queen, lazy tongues declare—*hail
has frozen over*, raging gods rain
wrath with sharp arrows of dry ice
to punish prejudice toward skin of darkness
in this frigid heart of the Bible Belt South.

Recollections of a boyhood in the South
flood a tired mind, recalling snow
jobs by cross-burning fools of darkness
wearing hooded choir robes—hailing
Satan as they packed black bodies on ice—
washing the blood away with dirty rain.
On the road a last time, nostalgia rains
on the brain, in this timeless, surreal, South.
Suddenly, a service station rest for iced
Coke, to numb my body cold as snow—
never to forget the cold trajectory—of the hail
of *KILL HOMOS*—blasting me out of darkness.

Rain, snow, hail, ice,
a tempest only befits my Southern goodbye—
as I escape the darkness of hate.

*Originally published in King Lear of the Taxi
(Advent Purple Press, 2006)*

KATHIE GIORGIO
The Story of the Literary Lion

I was around 23 years old when I first saw the episode called "The Book" from my favorite television show, *The Waltons*. At this point, the show was off the air, but was run in syndication on the Family Channel. I was hugely pregnant with my first child, and I was struggling to figure out what being a writer meant, now that I graduated with my degree and I was on my own and, amazingly, publishers were not breaking down my door to offer me a contract. In this episode, John Boy is discouraged when he's raked over the coals in his first serious creative writing workshop in college. John Boy's mother, Olivia, picks up on his discouragement. There is a new business in town called Majestic Press. She brings John Boy's collection of short stories to the publisher, and lo and behold, they accept it. Unfortunately, and too late, they find out that this is a vanity press, or a self-publisher. In the end, all they have is a box of fifty books and a bill for fifty dollars.

Before they know this, a professor stops John Boy on campus, and says, "Mr. Walton, you're getting to be a regular literary lion!" And later, Olivia says to her husband, "Imagine! Our son, a literary lion!"

At 23, and for all my life, I wanted to be a literary lion too. That phrase stuck with me.

In Manhattan, outside of the New York Public Library at Fifth Avenue and 42nd Street, there are two very well-known statues of lions, also known as Literary Lions. Since the 1930's, they've been named Patience and Fortitude.

I wanted to be a literary lion. I wanted to have patience and fortitude. These are so necessary to being a writer.

And so, this led to me always wanting to live in a place with a lion like Patience or Fortitude out front. A regal lion. A literary lion.

MY FIRST LITERARY LION

When we moved to our current home, I despaired of ever having a literary lion. Instead of living in a place steeped with history and classic architecture, we chose to move into a brand new, industrial style, modern live-where-you-work condo. My studio, AllWriters' Workplace & Workshop LLC, is on the first floor, and we live on the second and third floors. But on a shopping trip to Sam's Club, I came across a large fiberglass and resin sitting lion. He looked…very literary. So I brought him home and sat him in a little cutaway by our front door. He lasted about a year. I drove home one day and saw all these black pieces on the road. I wondered what they were. Then I saw that Literary Lion was missing. Someone attempted to steal him, but then must have grown tired of lugging him and dropped him, where he shattered. A part of me shattered too.

LITERARY LION #2

But I wasn't ready to give up. Sam's Club still had one left, on clearance since he was last summer's stock, and I brought him home. He actually lasted a few years. Then I found him sitting in the middle of busy North Avenue, just waiting to be hit by a bus. Again, abandoned by a thief, but at least this time, not dropped, but left for certain death. I brought him home and moved him into my classroom, where he sits to this day. I vowed to buy a concrete Literary Lion, who would be too heavy for a thief to take.

LITERARY LION #3

On June 15, 2011, I drove to O'Hare Airport, to pick up my daughter who was flying home from grad school in Florida. My middle son came with me. On the way home, we stopped at Garden Star

Garden & Art Gallery in Kenosha, WI. I passed this business many times and I always admired the amazing array of concrete statues on display. This time, I stopped, on a lion hunt.

And I found him. Little Literary Lion. He was smaller than #1 and #2, but he had an intelligent and benign face. He wanted a conversation, not a kill. And he was heavy as hell. My son and daughter both struggled to carry him and put him in his place. At that time, it was at the base of my hibiscus tree, in a pot outside the studio. During the summer, Little Literary sat in a jungle of potted flowers. And in the winters…well, he put up with the snow.

In April of 2014, I added a Little Free Library to the front of the studio. Little Literary took up his post under it. I often heard people talking to him as they looked through the books. Children in particular took delight in the little lion. Students spoke to him. He became a guidepost – "You'll know you're at AllWriters' when you see the concrete lion sitting under the Little Free Library." I gave him a pat on the head every time I filled the library with more books.

AND THEN…

Someone took Little Literary Lion during the winter of 2019. He disappeared. Whoever took him had to work as a team with someone. Someone also stole almost all the books in the Little Free Library. And this became about so much more than a missing garden statue.

I want to be a literary lion. I want to have patience and fortitude. And I want to believe in the common goodness of people.

That year, I turned 59, my last year of being in my fifties. One of my favorite books is Elizabeth Berg's *The Pull Of The Moon*. In it, a newly-turned 50-year old woman enters a time of personal grief. I read the book when I was 36, and I grieved for her. Then I read it again when I turned 50, and I grieved *with* her. There is a line in the book that says, "The season of losses is upon me." She was talking about her daughter going off to college, and the loss of many things for her physically as her body changed with age. The year my lion disappeared, my youngest daughter left to college and my oldest daughter moved away to Louisiana to teach at a college, both within a couple weeks of the other. My body had now dealt with cancer.

With turning 59 then and onward, now at 61, I ache with these losses, but my aches are particularly sharp around dreams. There are things I want to achieve that I haven't, and I know the likelihood decreases every year. Having a book made into a movie. Being on the New York Times Bestseller List. Having Oprah on my speed-dial.

And, you know, being a literary lion. Despite 11 books published, the 12th book being released this month, the 13th book being released in August of 2022, and the 14th book underway on my computer, and who knows how many stories and poems in magazines and anthologies… "Ms. Giorgio, you are becoming a regular literary lion!" has not happened to me.

It's been hard to think about.

And so the disappearance of Little Literary Lion, and the two before him, is like a metaphor to me. My literary lion disappeared. Just like the dream.

Add to this the feeling that the world has spun into such a negative cycle, I can barely breathe. I struggle daily to find the good. Just in the last week, there's been the Rittenhouse trial, a news article about a mother who sold her 13-year old daughter to a man so she could afford to party, a shooting, another shooting, more shootings, and of course, COVID. It feels never-ending.

And the books from my Little Free Library, meant to provide entertainment and solace to those who love to read, were stolen, along with my Little Literary Lion.

In this world, not even a little literary lion is safe.

So things felt pretty black for a bit.

On the AllWriters' Facebook business page, on Thursdays, I leave a tip for writers. Right about the time Little Literary Lion was stolen, I left a tip about how to make yourself pay attention to the positives, like acceptances, and turn away from the negatives, like rejections.

A week after the lion disappeared, I stood by my front door and looked at the empty space where Little Literary Lion used to be. My heart ached. And then I said, despite the clichés, "Healer, heal thyself. Practice what you preach."

Two people stole Little Literary Lion. Too many people to count tried to find him for me. The community shared my posts, the local paper did an article, and I received emails and phone calls of support, along with photos of a variety of concrete lions to see if they were mine. People shared tales of stolen gargoyles and angels, all of which were way more than gargoyles and angels.

Which meant then, and means now, that there are still more good people in this world than bad. That night, I lifted my eyes from the dark shadow beneath my Little Free Library and I looked at the light.

As for me? A couple years have passed since this happened. And did you see that one line in the middle of this? My twelfth book is coming out. My thirteenth book is coming out. My fourteenth is underway.

I've had patience. I've had fortitude. I still do. And I AM a literary lion. Despite no movie. Despite not being on the New York Times Bestseller List. Despite Oprah not having a clue who I am.

Let me tell you, she should.

AN ADDENDUM:

A few months after Little Literary disappeared, I found a new literary lion. He is also concrete, and he is stretched out on all four paws. Because of his length and size, he is (I hope) impossible to steal, His name is Little Leo Literary Lion. But…in July 2020, over a year past when Little Literary disappeared, I found him. He was in a resale shop in Lake Geneva, WI, about an hour away from my home. The owners of the shop wouldn't tell me where they got him from, just that he was sold to them. I bought him back and brought him home. He now lives safely on my third floor deck, where no one can take him again.

And no one can take my dreams either.

ROBERT GIBBONS
black and white on silver gelatin
(for Grey Villet)

in this city we are shown
black and white daguerreotype
will make you famous or a novelty
so to confront antebellum

which includes Jim Crow and miscegenation
which include seventy photographs
from a South African; it does not matter
in this pictures of an exhibition

relegated to the basement in weary blue
their lives spotted across the walls
like a Jackson Pollock on his birthday
there is a white man and a black woman

want to be married as segregated
as Virginia is to Maryland no wonder they
sought lady justice in Washington D.C.
as they had to cross back into Mason- Dixon

to the old dominion of place
where Martha Washington freed her slaves
where fear of an insurrection; where Prophet
dropped bread crumbs to created a trail

off the back of the stagecoach of George Washington
 paradox of slave holders, Presidents
slept in hay beds with black women
and dare not be buried in the same cemetery

saved the antiques after the War of 1812
and yet the stain of the fugitive slave and black codes
codes follow me to this room of weary blue
it steals away like Harriet did in the attic

and yes I paid twelve dollars to witness
this her-story; this time when racial integrity
was a shadow and an act; it was sedition
and treason and the challenge remains

as interracial couples and mix married mothers
kiss after they look at the trailblazer
their lives in pictorial obituary, she sitting
on the porch in putrid pink curlers

loving in her window; loving on her porch
loving in splendor; loving in her mirth
I ask what do you do when you walk across
the street and the light says stop

the glass frame of time square and the emptiness
is bare, it is the cameras and the action
its manners and the faction; the rise of the moment
some will still not own it.

TED GUEVARA
Refuge (70%)

On our counter, there's a bottle of isopropyl
alcohol. We had drilled a tiny hole on the cap.

The world would not miss the tiny evaporation,
would not heel to its disappearance,

considering the safety net it vows
upon our future scrapes and cuts,

like a freshly laundered sheet, conveniently
stuffed in the 16.9 fluid ounce bottle.

Our lives can afford rosy red, just not the pain
and the mystical, magical tour of accidents.

There is love in this world. You just need to focus
on the non-reddening. So, what if we're this

or that? There is no crime in our differences,
in our ability to make batter

without spilling milk on the counter. So?
There is independence

on a bored hole
for relief.

TED GUEVARA
Moron Moon

Let me shine between the mountains.
I'm sure my crescent will fit
the ragged valley, in time to reach
your preference heart.

Let me straighten the giddy light
on the river below, in time
to catch your benign fever, I zig
zag no more.

And all the songs, poems written, sang
about my following you,
I'm sure,
tomorrow, they would continue.

Tenderness is the key
to your anxiety.
Wild, I will tame
myself, in sync with your healing.

I'll shine before my age,
shoot high,
I must love you before atrophy reaches
careless plateau

The little moons in my head dance
to rhythm and beat. They are
guided and led
by maniacal little stars.

JOHN GUZLOWSKI
I Open My Hands

I open my hands
And see only my hands
The lines in my palms
That some say speak of fate
And love and misery
And the wonder to come
Some quiet morning in December
When the cold will silence the birds
And the asking in my palms.

And I close my hands
And see only my hands
The palms lost in them
The fate and love and wonder
Lost in this quiet December morning
As I turn to watch the leaves
Moving slowly in the wind

The birds are silent
The crows here last week are gone
Gone to the Carolinas
Where they hope to find some sun
I sit and watch the trees
As if they were my open hands.

FALEEHA HASSAN
No one said London is very cold!

Because I only sailed in the warmth of my city
And I never shook a snowman's hand
I didn't notice the wool socks or leather gloves
And because quoting is forbidden – in my mom's opinion -
I did not borrow a coat from Gogol *
Or anyone else
 I packed a bundle of my hot memories
And I left
....
The loving hearts shortened my farewell with fast beats
And reduced all their wishes to one "stay warm"
But before I could blink
Her watch came close to me
Shouted in my ear -: Big Ben*
I was terrified
When my stories froze.
The watch fell on her back laughing
When I told her:
 I was hiding in the pocket of my poem
 Warming by the fabric of letters.

....

*Gogol is the Russian novelist Nikolai Gogol, author of the coat story that novelist Turgenev said, "We all got out of Gogol's coat."

*Big Ben is the famous London clock that started in 1859 Clocks like Big Ben are large , watches are small and can be worn on the wrist.

FALEEHA HASSAN
New York

They do palmistry publicly here
In the streets
Over the terraces
And my hand is jailed in a glove
I stuff it in my coat's pocket and run.
Since you told me you don't read messages written by hand,
My hand streaks its lines.
I forgot to tell you that
It needs a tiny soft touch from you
Not a drop of Vaseline.
In the shadow of the skyscrapers
Longing is worse than cold.
Workers now repair the streets
 But I keep turning around in the crowd looking
at the features of someone who might look like you.
What if you could come from Najafi now?
Maybe you would help me to cross the street
Or
Be waving to the bus
I saved the warmth of my hand for you

DAMIAN WARD HEY
Jersey Archetype

In midnight scenes

a dog barks

once or maybe twice

in the space

between a stark moon

and our misery.

DAMIAN WARD HEY
Queens Archetypal – A Composite Poem of Eventually 100 Segments

I.

in midnight scenes

a dog barks

once or maybe twice

in the space

between a stark moon

and our misery

II.

monster is a hole

up in our face

disconnecting territories

a playground

swing set

with no swings

III.

tenements

disorganize before the sea

slow engines of decay

powered by vermin

machines of absent

tyrants

IV.

rockaway beach

destroys the world

one friday

all our castles gone

no shelter

sand

V.

imagine a home

without edges

a beach

without a shore

without

faith

VI.

monsters born

the disturbed visions

of our infant eyes

bury them

wait

forget

VII.

hear the

church bell strike

once

inscrutable

long disparate into many

souls

VIII.

horror

can you lounge

upon the beach

unhidden

as yourself frolicking

on vacation

IX.

sound

of the waves

bliss

gone

from the mind

the sea

X.

jackals

ride bikes around you

one calls out

yo man I like that red tie

no response

suffices

XI.

what is

that unseen dog

barking in the abject night

what to the monster

projected upon blacktop

implied by echoes

XII.

unsettled

by the interstices

of seasons

unhoused cold wet

we are present

unhinged

XIII.

but sing a song of joy

walls up

barriers refortified

we are a tribe

of wrought iron fences

and window guards

XIV.

chain link organism

tape worm

there is only one

anti linear

self replicating

con verging

XV.

you are made

of gutters and drainpipes

water as blood

shoes hung from the wires

spirit smoke

from an old mans cigar

XVI.

klavier

gentle fugue among

disorder

age of enlightenment

remnant

answering the waves

XVII.

much dancing

at low tide

among revealed things

watch the sea

slowly fill the foot prints

of absent dancers

XVIII.

uncounted patterns

in the cracks of sidewalks

could not quite be avoided

the search

for the birthplace of potholes

is ongoing

XIX.

do not haunt

where space is loud

and lean

do not fetch

a ghost from

a memory of tides

XX.

he brought

monsters to the new world

among desiring machines

but schizo you lack nothing

get up off the couch

go for a walk

XVI.

klavier

gentle fugue among

disorder

age of enlightenment

remnant

answering the waves

XVII.

much dancing

at low tide

among revealed things

watch the sea

slowly fill the foot prints

of absent dancers

XVIII.

uncounted patterns

in the cracks of sidewalks

could not quite be avoided

the search

for the birthplace of potholes

is ongoing

XIX.

do not haunt

where space is loud

and lean

do not fetch

a ghost from

a memory of tides

XX.

he brought

monsters to the new world

among desiring machines

but schizo you lack nothing

get up off the couch

go for a walk

LAYEBA HUMANITY
"Story Of The Footpath"

How many footprints pass.
I can't recognize their class.
I sometimes become the bed,
for a weary and poor person.
I am a witness of people's deeds,
Their old and modern version.

How many seasons do run.
Coolness of clouds, shine of sun.
While sleeping without a quilt,
some needy guys shiver in winter.
I wish I was a cold place in summer,
for those poor people who whimper.

How many reasons are there.
They really want a pure care.
I am sometimes mental asylum,
for the pious, mental, pure frame.
I'm sorry that I am unable to stop
illicit molesting happening to them.

How many scenes in one world,
as like lot meanings of one word.
Some have expensive cars,
someone is pulling a rickshaw.
Some throw food, some pick it up.
Is this the straight nature's law?

How many people are homeless.
On the other side some hopeless.
Flood washes away their homes,
to protect them I can't be the roof.
But ask me about their horrid lives,
I can show you their rare pain's proof.

How many outlaw procedures,
Cannot be cut with any scissors.
Oftentimes people litter and spit,
people break the rules of traffic.
I imagine, If I had hands and feet,
I would change the road's graphic.

How many misdoings are running,
atmosphere seems like cunning.
Beware while walking on footpath
that you are providing loss or gain.
Because the footprints may disappear
but their endless effects remain.

DIONNE D HUNTER
"ThanksGiving"

I recite this invocation in honor of the Ancestors
Both known and unknown
Millions of hardships overcome
Rivers swollen to the brink, with tears
Treacherous paths maneuvered with patient, laborious and thoughtful steps
With only the promise of the survival of your legacy pushing you onward
                              Thank you!
From the shores of the African continent, where the cradle of life was built,
and the first Kings and Queens reigned
                              Thank You!
In the name of your heartbreaking travels through the Middle Passage
And for the Blood, Sweat and Tears you spilled on the fields of the Americas
                              Thank you!
You, our Ancestors persevered
Grasping onto a fortitude that I deem transcendent
You planted seeds that took root and blossomed
Frantically you clawed at a system, that might have otherwise worn down the mightiest of your kindred
Your Faithfulness, Love and Dignity live on, bounding through limits placed on your bloodline by society
                              Thank you!
I now invoke the names of my maternal Grand and Great Grandmothers
Robina and Flora who blessed me with a love I did not appreciate until it was too late
                              Thank you!
And to my paternal Grandmother Mildred, who exhibited the strength of the Lioness
                              Thank you!
To my Mother and Father without your love, womb and seed I would never have had
the occasion to come into existence
Your Love and Guidance helped to mold me into the person I am today
                              Thank you!
Remembering our history is an expression of our gratitude for all the generations
that have come before us
Our Ancestors Bravery, Knowledge and Love fill our vessels to overflowing and allows us
all to even exist today
Allows us all to bathe in a Distinction not of our own making
We are built on Excellence honed on the Backs and Bones of mighty Men and Women
and until the end of all things and even then, we will show our thanks to the Ancestors
by bowing down on bent knee, while raising our hands to the heavens in honor of all their sacrifices
For all eternity and beyond! **T**o our Ancestors, **T**hanks, must be given!

RACHAEL IKINS
So Close: The Watcher

I was on the wall hunting flies in the sun
When the big black cars pulled up.
Men running with guns, doors slammed. Vibrations
traveled through my feet. I slid into shadow.

I was on the garage wall the day the white van drove in.
Young man, scabbed and sweaty left a handprint just below
my perch. Garage door rumbled up. Voices raised. Shouting.
I caught a fat fly that
day. It never saw me.

I saw the blonde girl many times. She played with small boys
 in the back yard.
She never let them catch lizards in jars or step on ants, squatting
 with them, three heads focussed on the way worker ants
carry their eggs to safety after rain floods
their burrow.

Sometimes he hit her.
I saw the man who came home without her leave,
my body still warmed by sunlight-soaked stucco, awake.
His movements those of a predator.

I see the television through their window, pictures of the blonde
 girl in faraway deserts where other lizards live. Maybe when he finished,
squeezed her neck so hard her feet didn't touch the ground, maybe she fell off
He threw her the

cliff into a wash below, limbs crooked as a tumbleweed.
Maybe some lizards sniffed her, lay against her, absorbed her body's floating
 heat. Maybe other lizards ate the flies that landed in her tangled hair,
mosquitoes that gathered around puddled blood.

I follow the sun on the house walls as day droops toward night.
There are cameras and microphones, but nobody sees me except
 an older woman watching the news far away.

She cries for the broken girl who died in plain sight while
everybody watched. Invisible, like a lizard blended into tree bark,
so many lost young women.
The words "Let it be."
inked on her arm.

LARRY JAFFE
Poet's Last Dance

Ever since I wrote my first word of poetry, I have felt captivated by the adventure to not only create a viable or beautiful poetry, but to make a major impact upon society, or what remains of it. In essence, I want to help create a new civilization built on the rocks and shoals of the current one. What a blessing to partake in it.

I started writing when I was 8 years old. I dressed up like a beatnik for Halloween. Words have been of great importance my entire life. As a poet, I have created my body of work based on several vital premises. The first was to be relevant. I think it is vital that artists be relevant to their readers and what is going on in the world. While it is perfectly alright to be lovey dovey and moon in June poetry, this was not my objective. I perceived myself as a poet – one who breathed in letters and breathed out words.

As a great fan of Woody Guthrie, I wanted my words to have the same type of relevance and impact. Printed on Woody's guitar were these words — This machine kills fascists. This simple phrase has inspired me throughout my life. These words kill Nazis, I thought to myself.

When Karen asked me what I wanted to write about, my instant reaction was to write a column or article about the role of a poet in the 21st Century. Poetry has been diminished and obfuscated throughout most of this century. I have even questioned the importance of poetry in today's modern world, where poets seem to be reading more to other poets and not the public at large. I have strived to change that.

Poetry haunts me. I think poetically. There is no getting around that. Poetry has been a calling, not a job. I am sure that most poets feel that way. The unemployed poet category would be enormous were it a job. I see poets as doctors of the soul!

This was exemplified on September 11, 2001. When 9/11 hit there was a huge resurgence of poetry, people looked at it for comfort during those trying times. I had been heavily involved in the Los Angeles poetry scene for many years back then. My compatriots (Don Deedon and Brandon Backhaus) hosted the incredible weekly readings at the infamous Moondog Café on Melrose Avenue no less. We packed that venue every Tuesday night. Folks were sitting on tables, under table and it was so interactive as audience members transformed themselves into poets. These readings were like church, so spiritual was the experience, with local poets and poets from all over the world appearing there. And there were folks there that just came to listen to our bards. It was immensely gratifying to see and hear live poetry exploding from the stage and have an appreciative audience. I then went on to be Poet in Residence at the Autry Museum of Western Heritage in Los Angeles.

But things have changed a lot since then. Poetry was no longer the go-to experience it once was. So many other things were competing for attention and truly it saddened me. It seemed like poetry was an oppressed artform and no one really seemed to care anymore. This was not a new experience for an old art. Poetry seems to lose its place in our civilization and then some historic moment takes place and the populace once again turn to poetry.

Nevertheless, in current times, poets became the" Rodney Dangerfields" of the art world. There was no or extraordinarily little respect. It felt like poets were writing for each other and not the world. Poetry was becoming a very insular society. Poetry was becoming verbal masturbation, and honestly, I was growing tired of it. This is how it appeared to me.

I was determined to write poetry that shook the rafters and make a better world. I wanted to create beauty with my words and change attitudes of intolerance and prejudice. I often felt like I was shouting to deaf ears. But still that ember burned deep inside me, looking for an outlet. I was still writing and publishing some to critical acclaim. I knew I needed to do more. Poetry readings had become rarer than diamonds and I knew I had to create a new reading series. I did and it was just starting to go great guns, nothing like I had in L.A. but still there was an audience of listeners as well as poets. Then COVID – 19 hit and well, that was that.

I love the feeling of a live reading. It is so spontaneous and yes, so freakin alive! I don't think it could be simulated on Zoom, etc. If you have never experienced a live poetry reading, put it on your to-do list as it is a fantastic experience. It is the only art form where the interactivity between artist and audience is not just profound, it is interchangeable. The audience member suddenly slips into the persona of the artist then resumes their position in the audience. It is a sublime experience and I hope to get our reading going again in March.

All this reminiscing leads us to this day in January where a young poet made her international debut at the presidential inauguration. Putting politics to the side (which is where they belong in my humble opinion) Amanda Gorman put on quite a show and made me so proud of her. Her voice rose to the occasion. And again, putting petty politics to the side, she created a feeling of unity and love and community. Then she went on to read another poem at the Super Bowl! Imagine that, a poet reading at the Super Bowl. I still cannot get over it! Poetry is on people's lips again. And I still write my words proud to be a poet.

This then is the role of the poet – to speak up for the voiceless, to interpret the future and create a new tomorrow. This is the role of a poet, to roll back the past to heal it, to cut through the jargon of the present and speak of the future honoring humanity.

PAVOL JANIK
THE TOUCH
Translated into English by Smiljana Piksiades

Landscape of a country of miracles.
Beds of the bankless rivers of salty water.
Under them flows a boiling metal.
A female trunk is smouldering in my arms.

(1981)

PAVOL JANIK
IT IS BEHIND THE DOORS
Translated into English by Smiljana Piksiades

All internal voices squeak
and complain about a chilly night.

Armless and wingless,
endlessly simplified moon
descended
from the sky
and spread itself
right in our garden.

It is already making his first acquaintances.

(1981)

JAKE ST. JOHN
On My Way To Work

Morning mist rising
from the river
encircles the bridge
in a ring of fog

lingers
over the road
like midnight
kisses left
on my lips

onward
through
haze filled
highway

entering
the day
thoughts exit
the commute

the memory
of your touch
travels
the boulevards
of my heart

here
a smile and
coffee
is enough

the seconds
set like the sun
on the evening road
that eventually returns
me to you.

ZANETA VARNADO JOHNS
A Different Kind of Diversity

One student tentatively walked alone to school
Another had little sleep—awakened by nightmares
One hurts from sleeping in the cold outdoors
Another has not eaten since yesterday's free lunch
One was touched all night in all the wrong places
Another hides bruises for fear of scolding
One child is ashamed of his family's heritage
Next to him a girl hides her ethnic lunch
In the corner sits a boy who feels like a girl
Staring at a girl who feels like a boy
One child feels worthless as repeatedly told
Another won't speak because of her accent
One child grieves his beloved pet
Another lost a sibling during a traffic stop
One child is hoping to soon be adopted
Another is surrounded by endless love
One witnessed her parents taken away in handcuffs
Another worries about his mother's black eye
One child limps and dreads ridicule
Another is bullied but afraid to report
One is fretful because her friends ignore her
Another hides and listens for gunshots
One was promoted although he cannot read
Another is autistic, trapped in her own mind
One was told that he is better than others
Others were taught that we all have value
Many are prepared and ready to learn
Some are not equipped yet eager to learn
All children are worthy of equal investment
their minds wide open
their hearts full of love
Every child deserves a safe bright future
Every child is our future's best shot at peace
The right teacher entrusted with this
classroom of children
will greet them with compassion
will meet them at their needs
will empower them with knowledge
will encourage them to read
An empowered empathetic teacher
can break the cycle of hatred and fear.

pj johnson Poet Laureate of the Yukon
dwight

dwight was born bi-racial
at a time
when it wasn't alright
to be bi-racial

dwight was born gay
at a time
when it wasn't alright
to be gay

dwight's mother
abandoned him
because she didn't want
a bi-racial child

dwight's foster parents
ridiculed him
because they didn't want
a gay son

dwight's friends
beat him
because they didn't want
a fag for a friend

dwight jumped off a bridge
in vancouver in 1969
because he didn't want
to live

he was my big brother
his name was dwight
all lives matter

Graphic by pj johnson Poet Laureate of the Yukon

pj johnson Poet Laureate of the Yukon
it was the land

no one knew the evil men could do
behind closed doors
no one spoke of it
no one said sorry
and in the end
it was the land
the very land itself
that spoke

it was the land
that carried the secrets
that knew the truth
that yielded a million sorrows
that stopped us like a thunderbolt
in the streets.
god forgive us
the whispers were true

it was the land that spoke for thousands
denied a life. denied a family
denied a mother tongue
and as our grief-filled days
stretched out before us
like a blanket of fear
from the land of the Mi'kmaq to *Haida* Gwaii
we were numb with disbelief

for it was the land
the very land itself
that spoke to us in the darkness
in the sacred smoke of our ancestors
and in the voices of our children
who whispered on the wind
guiding us
showing us the way

telling us
there will be a time
for coming together
as a nation. as a people. and as a family
to celebrate now
and lift our brothers and sisters
as never before
our tears are never far from the surface

it always gets darker before the light comes back

JILL SHARON KIMMELMAN
Contemplation Of A Phoenix In Flight

On wings of doves you begin
in freedom you have found an extraordinary voice
celebration of your journey's path

In tranquility your words returned

Whispers within your heart first denied
incessant gentle nudges avoided
until you could no more   words
their impassioned pleas
than you could stop
your heart from beating
your lungs from breathing
your pen from bleeding

Every word created sonnets and stanzas
awaited, welcomed, inspiration accepted

Your declaration
drafted in tears, haunted by fears
an affirmation of strangers

celebrate freedom earned, lessons learned

Like the lotus, your greatest gifts grew greater
in the ooze of mud

A magnificent Phoenix, plumes of every hue
grandest of dreams now yours to pursue

A vibrant blossom ablaze with fiery gems
your magical words
most beautiful Phoenix soaring
proud, strong, tall, no doubts at all
most magnificent of birds
most beautiful of all.

from the collection "You Are The Poem", Jill Sharon Kimmelman

SUSAN KSIEZOPOLSKI
Edge of Our Days

Listen to our fizzling days
the message they bring
wrapped in the muffled sensibility that is calling
to comfort us
imploring us
to answer for ourselves.

As we forge our way around the scalding sun
in our troubled times
there is no retirement from our living
our restless inner compass labours
guides us
out from the edge of our life.

May the fading end of our being
de wrapped in endless rest
earned before the blazing beginning
of season's end.

JANET KOZACHEK
A White Cat Comes In

A calculus of squares and triangles bound within and without a hoop
overflowed into a flat land of geometric patterns.
Blue seeped into white and a sprinkling of white settled onto blue
- like snow on a distant mountain.
Geese flew by in red along a meandering periphery,
marking the ends of territories.
A cat sauntered in
altering the balance of borderline divisions in a square space.
The quilter gazed upon his feline presence,
as he tucked his lithe little arms beneath his delicate body.
White folded onto blue as pink blossomed into white,
like young rosy lips that kissed the silver hairs of winter.

From *A Rendering of Soliloquies, Figures Painted in Spots of Time*. Finishing Line Press. February, 2022.

"Double Blind Placebo Affect" by Janet Kozachek

"A White Cat Comes In" by Janet Kozachek

W. RUTH KOZAK
Byron in Greece

At the corner of Lysikrattis and Vironos Streets in Athens Plaka, stands a choreographic monument awarded to a choir at a Festival for Dionysos in ancient Athens' Dionysos Theatre. Once, next to this monument, the last of its kind in Athens, was a French Capuchin convent. The poet, George, Lord Byron, stayed here when he was in Athens. At that time, the panels between the columns of the monument had been removed, so Byron used it as his study and wrote part of Childe Harold here in 1810-11. This was once the theatre district of ancient Athens, so it seemed appropriate that the flamboyant poet should choose to spend his time there. In Greek, "Vironos" means "Byron" and this is Byron's street. I used to live there and spent much of my leisure time at the little milk shop, now a posh coffee shop, at that corner. The convent was destroyed in a fire, but there's an inscribed monument on the spot where it once stood honouring Byron. His presence always seemed near.

The street adjacent, is Shelley Street, named for his poet colleague Percy Byce Shelly who tragically drowned in Italy. Both poets are honoured in Greece, especially Byron, who became a national hero when he joined the Greek resistance movement during the War of Independence.
While in Athens he often lodged with a widow, whose daughter, Theresa Marcri is celebrated in his poem *The Maid of Athens*. The house where he lived in the district of Psiri at Odhos Pyias Theklas, is marked with a plaque. There are traces of him in various locations. If you visit the Temple of Poseidon at Sounion you will see his name carved in the marble steps. *Sunium's marbled steep, where nothing save the waves and I may hear our mutual murmurs sweep.*

I have visited many of the places where Byron lived and can understand how the beauty and serenity of the Greek landscape inspired him. Byron wrote many poems about Greece including the famous *"Isles of Greece"*

The isle of Greece! The isles of Greece!
Where burning Sappho loved and sung,
Where grew the arts of war and peace,--
Where Delos rose and Phoebus spring!

Byron first visited Greece in 1809, landing in the town of Parga. From there he went north to Ioannina where the infamous Ali Pasha held sway. While there he visited the Pasha who had an even shadier reputation with women than the poet. Ali Pasha, like Bryon, also appreciated beautiful young men. He was enchanted by Byron, noting his delicate small ears "the mark of good breeding". It was during his stay in Ioannina that Byron began his autobiographical narrative poem, *Childe Harold's Pilgrimage*, which commemorated his meeting with Ali Pasha who had lavished hospitality on him. Byron knew though that behind Ali's deceptively friendly countenance were *"deeds that lurk"* and *"stain him with disgrace"*. Athens. While at Ioannina he loved to swim out to a small island in the lake. In spite of being born with a club foot, Byron was a skilled swimmer and once swam the across Hellespont from Troy. To this day they hold swimming meets there to remember him.

Yet are thy skies as blue, thy crags as wild;
Sweet are thy groves, and verdant are thy fields,
Thine olive ripe as when Minerva smiled,
And still his honey'd wealth Hymettus yields;
There the blithe bee his fragrant fortress builds,
The freeborn wanderer of thy mountain-air;
Apollo still thy long, long summer gilds,
Still in his beam Medeli's marbles glare:
Art, Glory, Freedom fail, but Nature still is fair.
                                  -*Childe Harold's Pilgrimage*

Byron traveled the country extensively often visiting the islands. On Lefkada (Levkas) Childe Harold *saw the hovering star above Leucadia's far projecting rock of woe"*. This was at the site of ancient Leukadas, a precipitous cliff 200 feet high where there was once a Temple to Apollo. It was here, known today as "Sappho's Leap" that the lyric poet Sappho tragically committed suicide by jumping off the cliff.

In 1823, apparently bored with his extravagant life in Italy, Byron sailed to Spain and Malta before finally returning to Greece. This voyage is detailed in his poem *Sailing with Byron from Genoa to Cephalonia*. From Preveza he went north to Parga

He lived for awhile on the island of Kefalonia (Cephalonia) in the tiny village of Metaxata, near Argostoli, where he enjoyed exploring the ruins of a Venetian castle at Ayios Yeoryios, once the Venetian capital of the island.

During his travels around Greece, Byron not only grew to love the country but was also impressed with the moral tolerance of the people. He became involved in the rebellion against the Turks, joining forces with Alexandros Mavrokordatos, the leader of the forces in western Greece to take part in the War of Independence. In spite of Byron's lack of military training, together they planned to attack the Turkish-held fortress of Lepanto at the mouth of the Gulf of Corinth. The Greek struggle against the ruthless Turks was supported by many intellectuals and poets like Lord Byron who volunteered to fight and become leaders of the revolution. They were known as the *Philhellenes* (friends of the Greeks). Although many became disillusioned by the pettiness and greed of the Greek *klefth* leaders others, like Bryon, took up the cause, arriving in Messolonghi , a squalid little port on the Gulf of Corinth, the western outpost of the resistance movement against the Ottomans. He was greeted with a 21 gun salute. In spite of despairing *"in this realm of mud and discord"* he donated 4000 pounds of his own money to prepare the Greek fleet for sea service and employed a fire master to prepare artillery as well as paying the Souliot soldiers who were reputedly the bravest of the Greek resistance fighters.

On Suli's rock, and Parga's shore,
Exists the remnant of a line
Such as the Doric mothers bore:
And there, perhaps, some seed is sown,
The Heracleidan blood might own.
Trust not for freedom to the Franks—
They have a king who buys and sells;
In native sword and native ranks,

The only hope of courage dwells:
But Turkish force and Latin fraud
Would break your shield, however broad.

During the spring of 1824, Byron fell ill but continued to carry out his duties. During his recovery he was unfortunately caught in a rainstorm and came down with a violent cold. Unfortunately this was aggravated by the bleeding insisted on by the doctors which may have caused sepsis. He slipped into a coma and died on April 1824 at the age of 37.

The Greeks considered him a hero and buried his heart at Messolonghi where there is now a small museum containing Byron artefacts. He remains were sent to England but refused burial in Westminster Abby and were instead placed in the vault of his ancestors new Newstead. It wasn't until 145 years after his death, that a memorial to Byron was placed on the floor of the Abbey.

In Greece, he was still revered, and a beautiful monument to him held in the arms of an angel who stands at the edge of the National Garden in Athens. Each time I'm in Athens I visit it and think of the life and poetic words of this exceptional and intriguing man of literature.

WEB SITES ABOUT BYRON IN GREECE
http://www.ahistoryofgreece.com/revolution.htm
http://englishhistory.net/byron/life.html
http://www.dailymail.co.uk/news/article-1078582/Greece-hails-Lord-Byron-hero-dedicates-day-celebration-name.html
The Messolonghi Byron Society: http://rea.teimes.gr/byronlib/

MESSALONGHI: The house where Byron lived was destroyed in WW II and there is a small memorial garden at the site. There is a small museum devoted to the revolution on central Platia Botsari (Mon-Fir 9 am – 1.20 pm and 4-7 pm. Sat & Sun 9am – 1 pm & 4 -7 pm. There is a small collection of Byronia on the ground floor. In the Kipos Iroon (Garden of Heroes) there is a statue of Byron beside the tomb of Souliot commander Markos Botsaris, erected in 1881.

R. NIKOLAS MACIOCI
Dandelions and Grief

Dandelions, yellow dowsing rods,
turn toward the sun. Grief, gray as gravel,
takes me away from where I want to be.
Brahms, nightingales, mourning doves
make sounds of grief. Dandelions give
wine, salad, grow old fast. They raise
their heads against summer's first blue sky.
Grief scuttles across the face of religion,
scarring rituals of belief, settles in
Cassandra's eyes where there is nothing
but doubt. In a field, corn-colored dandelions
catch fire from orbiting day, decay to a seeded
fuzzball breeze catches in its net, and seeds fall
to earth like stars. Grief Paints walls of the heart
with pain. If grief had knees, it would fall down
on them, beg to be noticed. Dandelion seeds
tear from stems, drift in air, miniature parachutes.
In the hand they disintegrate like ash, delicate
as anonymity.

I once saw a young boy take a bouquet
of dandelions to a grave. He placed
them at the bottom of the tombstone.
I was sitting several yards away on a bench,
heard words that could have been a prayer
or a scream of insanity over loss. I saw
his surprise when I went to the pump
and brought him a bucketful of water
for his flowers. He thanked me, called me mister.
Beyond that, we didn't talk. I started
toward my car, turned back and noticed
the dandelions, in spite of the water,
had already begun to wilt. The last thing
I saw from my car was the boy
smashing his fist into the tombstone.

R. NIKOLAS MACIOCI
Circus, 1950

Ringling Bros. and Barnum Baily circus
used to pitch its tent in a field
next to Red Bird Stadium on Mound Street.
One summer, when I was nine,
I shook my dad from a drunken sleep,
begged him to take me to the circus.
He swayed, staggered into his clothes,
and we trekked several blocks to the bus stop .

On the corner of the second block, he wanted
a quick beer from Leo's Bar.
I slumped onto a stool, watched colors change
on the jukebox. He clutched the bar to raise himself,
and we started off again.

After boarding a bus, he leaned his head
against a window and slept. At our destination,
I thumped him on the back. For a few seconds,
he seemed confused.

The show lasted two hours. Then, he bought me
a chameleon on a short leash which the vendor pinned
to my shirt. Dad, as if by alcoholic radar, spotted
a bar across the street. He entered, and the lizard
and I followed.

Dad ordered a Stroh's for himself and a 7Up for me.
The lizard and I took off to the restroom downstairs.
The lizard had turned the color of my brown shirt.
I studied my face in the mirror, saw a desire to escape.

We climbed back upstairs to Doris Day singing
"teacher's pet, I wanna be a teacher's pet,"
and I understood at that moment her need to belong
to someone, somewhere safe and secure.

ANGIE MACK
Flow*

I love *flow*……. now *go*!
I *swim* for the flow.
I like *jazz* for the flow.
I like *dresses* for the flow.
Crazy *hair* that flows.
*Wat*ercolors flow
and the *wind* when it blows.
*Every*body knows
mainly *Mari*lyn Monroe.
Baby turn up the car *ra*dio.
I *hear* a whistle in the *air*-io.
A pe*cu*liar sound that's so *rare*-io.
*Syn*copated scen*a*rios.
Three little birds out my *win*dow.
Fee*l*ings flow.
My *flow*ers grow
while *whim*sical weeds
steal the show.
My *hat* flies off.
There it goes!
I *used* to be teased
For *hav*ing a fro.
*Phone*mes riff.
Allitera*t*ions dance.
*Fan*cy phrases.
Spont*a*neous laughs.
*Photo*graphic phases
*cap*ture the faces.
Ex*press*ionism *run*ning high.
*O*pen circuits
*sa*ving time.
Int*ui*tive physics
my *se*cret in life.
*Liv*ing fluid
makes me phly.
With*out* restraints
it's *eas*y to fly!

*emphasize italics

"He Leads Me Beside Still Waters" by Angie Mack
taken at the Beyond Van Gogh Milwaukee Exhibit, 2021.

"Artists and Brothers" by Angie Mack
taken at ArtfindZ in Hartford Wisconsin, 2021

"Little Pink Anderson Visits the Grafton House of Blues with Blu" by Angie Mack taken in Grafton, Wisconsin while working on Little Pink's Autobiography, 2021

MIKE MATTHEWS
Blue Man

The Blue Man sitting in a blue chair in the dark heard the telephone ring.
The telephone rang in the dark. The telephone rang.
The Blue Man made of glowing light touched the telephone as it rang.
The Blue Man held the receiver to the ill-defined line of his ear.

After a pause, Blue Man breathed blue light into the mouth piece.
The telephone translated the light:
    Hello. Who's there?
Blue Man heard:
    Am I speaking to the person who makes decisions?

Blue Man paused. Glowing blue light floated into the phone
like dark blue smoke:
    Why are you asking that question?
Blue Man heard:
    I'm calling to offer a magnificent deal
    my cleaning company is poised to give you.
    For half the price it would normally cost,
    we will clean the expectations off your floor.
Blue Man asked:
    The what?
He heard:
    The expectations that you walk on every day.
    We will rid your home of them.
    Will you elect to let us clean your home?
Blue Man said:
    I don't know of anything on my floors like that.
He heard:
    Studies have shown that most homes are filthy
    with expectations that have never been cleaned away.
    At your convenience, I can send a crew
    to restore your floors, the very foundation of your home,
    to the luster and shine they were meant to have.
Blue Man said:
    I am sure that I don't have any of those on my floors.
The voice on the telephone asked:
    What is your name, sir?
Blue Man said:
    Blue Man.
The voice said:
    Well, blue sir,
    do you ever expect anything?
Blue Man thought.

Blue Man said:
> *I expect to one day to hear a synchronized beat*
> *of the single wing of every flying insect and bird.*

The voice said:
> *I see…*
> *Well, sir, I cannot see*
> *why you would pass on this opportunity.*
> *Can I count on a time for us to come visit you?*

Blue Man said:
> *I should have to think about it, sir.*

He heard:
> *I'll leave my number.*
> *How does that sound to you?*

Blue Man said:
> *Like red light.*

He heard:
> *What?*

He said:
> *Sounds fine. Good night.*

After Blue Man returned the phone's hook to its cradle,
he slowly faded into darkness and fell asleep.
One of the back legs of the blue chair faded away, too.

JOAN MCNERNEY
Luck

Wearing designer clothes
and sleek jewelry,
she traipses along willy nilly
throwing golden kismet
wherever whimsy calls.

Some think Luck chooses their
goodness or hard work. Perhaps
they were blessed at birth?

The wise know luck wears a
visor tripping over herself
favoring both mean and lazy.

Luck has a toxic twin called
Misfortune covered with
gloom. Dressed in dusty
rags, stupor-like he selects
unsuspecting victims.

Stomping helter skelter
clutching the throats of
both meek and mighty.

Everybody who gets in his way
will be pushed down, their
muffled cries barely heard.

KARLA LINN MERRIFIELD
Étude 4-23: Embodiment on the Day I Changed Strings for a Second Time

I want to hold somebody
I want to hold somebody
I want to hold some body

I want to kiss somebody
I want to kiss somebody
I want to kiss some body

I want to breathe on somebody
I want to breathe on somebody
I want my breath on some body
I want my sweat on somebody's hands
I want my tears on somebody's brow
I want my dew on some body

—and his on mine—but—
but it shall not be *now*
no matter my wants   his   yours

so I want my fingers rippling somebody
so I want my thighs cradling somebody
so my heart's wants lift now some body: my guitar.

FRANK MOTTL
The Unusual Case of Ephemera Higgins

Ephermera lives from charcoal black burnt toast to charcoal black burnt toast, that, and her friend who occasionally has intercourse with the little bell that hangs in his cage. They keep her going from long year to long year.
She wakes by sound. The little bell tinkling in the cage as the budgie humps the metal thing: tinkle, tinkle it goes.
"You dirty little birdie," she says.
"Tweet, chirp to you to," says the bird.
"Don't be cheeky."
The budgie turns, flips up his tail feathers, and a little round, white drop of poop comes out.
"Oh," Ephemera exclaims, "there'll be no black toast for you, dirty bird, Dirty Bird."
She cracks the kitchen curtain and peeks outside.
"Boy's coming today, Dirty Bird," she says.
"Chirp," says Dirty Bird.
She cranks up the setting on the toaster and waits.
"No milk toast for you," she says to the toaster.
The kitchen smokes. The toaster protests, wishes for nice, white milk toast.
The ceiling clouds and swirls, she inhales and Dirty Bird flaps in his cage.
A knock at the door!
She hurries, shuffles across the linoleum, and opens the door with a grand swirl of black smoke. It's Frankie.
"You wanted your windows done today," he says.
"Oh, yes, expecting you," she says, "step ladders in the shed, start here, in the kitchen."
Frankie on the ladder cleans the window, on the outside, then remains and waits.
Ephemera's there, glasses on the end of her old nose, tap, tap, taps with her index finger.
"Here, here," she says.
Tap, tap, there, tap, tap, here, and he sprays and washes till she's happy.
"Fifty cents an hour," she says, "three hours that's a buck fifty."
She tinkles the change in Frankie's hand.
"Cheap, rich old bag," he thinks.
He smiles.
"Thanks, see you next week."
She walks to town, gets the post, a letter! She goes to her bench and opens it right there, an invitation, my name? What? Come to Texas, it says. A convention, people with my name? A contest, a poem? How exciting. She thinks, waits on the bench, then thinks of a doughnut but decides not, too excited, so continues home.
"Dirty Bird, Dirty Bird," she exclaims shaking the invitation, "a contest, I need to write a poem about you," she says.
Dirty Bird flaps in the cage.
"We need to think, out you come."
Dirty Bird flies around the house and settles on Ephermera's shoulder. She is sitting at the kitchen table, pen and paper in hand.
"Now what do you think?"

"The poem silly, what should I write, after all it's about you."
Dirty Bird flutters on her shoulder.
"Don't you dare poop," she says.
Dirty Bird squats and scoots his neck in acquiescence, and peers at the paper.
"Good, now let's see: *Into my morning head I hear a tinkling bell it sounds quite near.*"
Dirty Bird chirps, and is soft as he tits her neck.
"I know, I do have a knack for it," she says.
"I get up, my house coat on to see the ruckus cage within
"Chirp, too-witt, too-woo."
"Yes, yes."
"A little bird chirps his song, I feed burnt toast to aid along."
"Chirp, chirp, tweeter-too."
"Yes, I see, how's this, *I hum with yellow bird with glee, for it is my best company.*"
She twists and looks at Dirty Bird from the corner of her eye.
"You are my best."
"Coo-Kooo."
"Sometimes he likes to fly quite free, yet always comes home to abide with me."
"Chirp, tweet," says Dirty Bird flapping his wings.
"I like it too."
"Tomorrow I'll post it off, and if I win, I'm off to Texas! You too!"
Dirty Bird flaps excitedly.
The long days are longer because Dirty Bird and Ephemera are waiting patiently for the post, and one day, it arrives.
She sits on her bench. Her hands shake as she opens the letter, it says:

THE EPHEMERA HIGGINS CONVENTION
Dear Ms. Higgins,
Please be advised that your poem, 'Yellow Bird Swagger' is one of the finalists in the contest. Kindly return this letter with your endorsement and we will complete your registration as finalist. We look forward to seeing you there!
Yours in Service,
Ephemera B. Higgins,
Head of Selection Committee,
Amarillo, Texas

"How officious," she thinks.
I've won, I've won, I've won! Then halts herself aware that she's only a finalist. The winner won't be announced until the convention. She rushes home to tell Dirty Bird. It's quiet in the house, Dirty Bird must be napping, so she is soft with her footsteps, going in the side door and places her purse on the bed, and clasps her wonderful letter.
"Yoohoo, Dirty Bird, look what I have," gaily and musical.
But there is no chirping or tweeting or too-witt-too-wooing, instead, at the bottom of the cage lies Dirty Bird, there, on the cage floor surrounded by little white poops, like a little angel.
She sighs.
"Time for a strong cup of tea," she says to the kettle.

A dainty cuppa, then cleans her kitchen again, lays on the couch, and sleeps, warm and comfy.
She wakes to a knock, knock, knocking on the door. It's Frankie.
"Hi Ms. Higgins, you told me to keep knocking if no answer, today's the day for the edges."
 "Yes, right, not today, but come tomorrow, I have something special for you to do."
Ephemera puts dead Dirty Bird in a shoe box, but it's too big, so finds one smaller. She places the bird soft in the bottom on crepe paper, and thinks she hears a small chirp as she puts the lid on. A tear pierces her eye.

MARK MURPHY
Contemporaneity or Marx est Mort

All Marxisms have become imaginary.
– Étienne Balibar

No class struggle. No mode of production. No proletarian revolution.
No reification. No interpellation. No impenetrable hieroglyphics.
No metaphysics. *No lingua franka.* No capitalism. No market economy.
No libertarian conservatism. No neoliberalism. No deregulation.
No privatization. No IMF. No World Bank. No GATT. No Global Top
100 Companies. No market capitalization. No globalization.
No trade barriers. No individualization. No right to healthcare.
No interventionism. No neocolonialism. No cultural imperialism.
Pas de laissez-faire. Pas d'expression libre. Pas de liberté de choix.
No *de facto* one-party state. No New World Order. No power elites.
No oligarchs. No gradualism. No dominionism. No white supremacism.
No Brave New World Order. No neo-Nazism. No eliminationism.
No humane Marx. No scientific Marx. No real Marx. No Politology.
No timely Marx. No untimely Marx. No imaginary Marx.
No anarcho-syndicalism. No anarcho-socialism. No Occupy movement.
No discordance of time. NO PCF. No FG. *Pas de marxisme français.*
No Henri Lefebvre. No Georges Politzer. No Paul Nizan.
No Jean Paul Sartre. No Raymond Aron. No Lucien Goldman.
No Roger Garaudy. No Louis Althusser. No Althusserianism.
No Andre Gorz. No Kostas Axelos. No Guy Debord. No Lucien Seve.
Pierre Macherey. No André Tosel. No Etienne Bolibar. No Daniel Bensaid.
No plurality of Marxes. No unified Marx. No post-Marxist Marx.
No contemporary subjugation. No contemporary alienation.
No contemporary inequality. No contemporary epistemology.
No *conflict of subjectivations.*
  Pas de justice sociale. Pas d'iniquité.
Pas de Jacques Derrida. Pas de déconstructionnisme. Pas de Jean-Marie Benoist.

Pas de Marxisme du 20eme Siècle.
Pas de Marxisme du 21e Siècle.
Pas de Spectres de Marx.

Marx est Mort. Marx est Mort. Marx est Mort. Marx est Mort. Marx…

ELAINE NADAL
Eyes

Grandmother used to talk about having peace within a storm.
It was an idea from one of her favorite hymns.
I particularly found no enjoyment in the melody
but appreciated the sentiment.
My storm would end when the sun
was no longer out of reach,
and I obtained the freedom to be.

I'd stare at the window, hoping to see beyond--
to travel across.
I was not allowed to go out.
Mother was not allowed to go out either.
Brother went out and received no beating,
so I looked forward to thunder and rain.
There was no escapade to miss,
and the house was less wearisome.

My storm would grow many legs and flee,
but before shrinking and growing legs,
it grew scales and many heads.
Its eyes still appear in the stillness of a season.
They have followed me across the beach
to the little house I rent.

Today, I am old enough to be.
Today, a hurricane strengthens before arriving in the morning.
The orange-blue sky has no signs of chaos yet.
I watch the sun go down and think of my grandmother—
dead in her bed-- with her eyes open and no teeth,
defaced by a storm she kept to herself,
and I do not pray for peace within.
I pray simply for peace.

ANDREW NAJBERG
The Glory of Steve

Steve thrust his ball peen hammer high towards the sky, his forehead sweating, his mouth tight. The afternoon sun caught the polished, stainless steel head, and it was almost as if he held a sliver of the sun. This was it. This was his moment.

The watermelon before him would be shattered open with one mighty stroke, spilling its red water-blood and black seeds all over the picnic table.

Steve bellowed at the top of his lungs as the hammer's ball splintered straight down into to the wood, cracking the whole surface, and he whipped his head about as pulp chunks and rind burst across his face.

His children watched in awe and terror as the stroke fell. Marcie turned ashen white, except the translucent pink spots where juice spray pocked her cheeks and forehead. She closed her hand around her purse and drew it to herself like a newborn.

The parents of the other members of the soccer team slowly got up from their benches, shielding their sons and daughters with their arms, and they backed slowly towards the parking lot as they fished car keys out of pockets and purses. A low muttering arose. Awe, Steve knew.

Still in his striped shirt and drinking a can of orange soda, the referee glanced nervously to the whistle on the trunk of his car, contemplating the distance and whether the whistle would stop actions here as well as in the field. The game was over, and any authority he still held would be an illusion, a habit.

Steve's daughter tugged at his wife's skirt hem, eyes wide, breathing shallow.

"Jesus, Steve," Marcie said, "You're scaring Suzy. You're scaring the whole team."

"Scaring them?" Steve said. "How do you think I feel?"

Steve thrust his fingers into the watermelon half and shoved a fistful into his own mouth before flinging another chunk at one of the retreating parents.

"You see this?" Steve roared. "This watermelon is my heart!"

Steve threw the fistful of pulp to his feet.

"And this, this is what Marcie did to my heart last night."

Steve ground his heel into the already obliterated fruit.

A woman cried out.

A man darted behind the park dumpster, and poked his head out around the corner.

A dog barked through an open SUV window. A little boy crouched behind the Suburban's wheel held his mother's cell phone to his ear.

"Steven, this is not the place!" Marcy whimpered.

"God forbid the neighbors know," Steve said. With a surge of seemingly supernatural strength, he held the hammer haft in one head, the head in the other, and snapped the tool in two.

Thunder in the distance infected the ground under their feet. Paper cups rattled. A plastic fork fell off the table and clattered against the bench. In the distance, sirens wailed like banshees.

Steve knew there was no going back. He threw the remains of his hammer at the nearest trash can where it clattered uselessly against the plastic. Then, he grabbed his collar and tore his shirt in half, revealing his hairy shoulders and the strange mole just above his left nipple. Then, he vaulted over the picnic table and ran through the first spattering of rain towards the woods. Through the woods cardinals and ravens swooped through the trees, and the river ran its course. At the river's end, thousands of miles of ocean. Near the end of the continental shelf, a vast, dying reef. Perhaps there among the fading coral, he would find the strength to start himself anew.

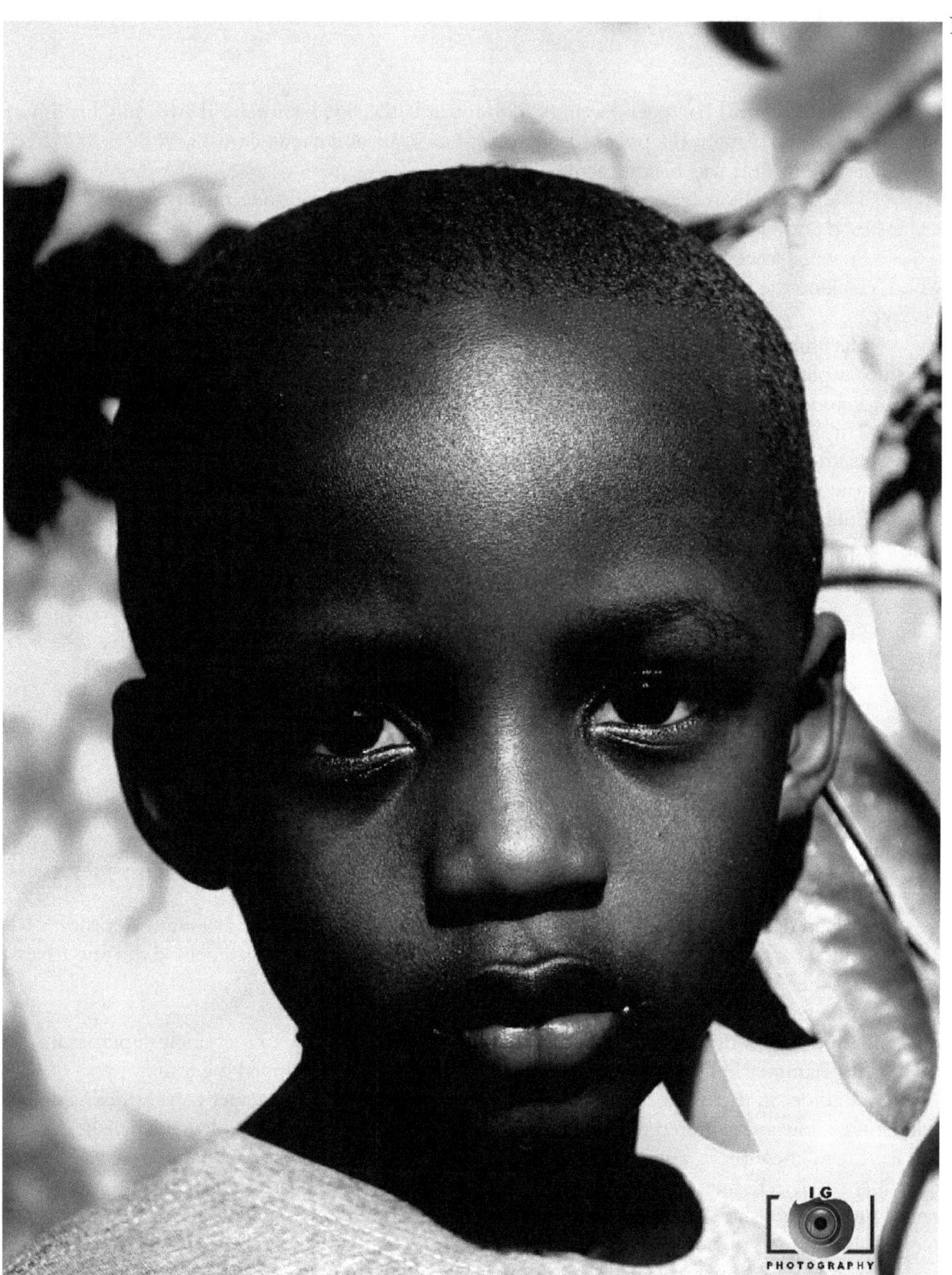

Photo by Aji Ndumbeh Jobe

XRISA NICOLAKI
The Gift of Pneuma

I laid an honorary wreath
I prayed for your name
in the church I lit a candle
and I started my frenetic
and ecstatic dance
on Dionysus rhythm

and I said

Heaven and Hell
you my Earth and you my Sky
barefoot I run
away from the temple
crying I raised my head up high

and I asked:

oh you, Adam's descendants
which is your original sin?

Life is here and so is Death

CHAD NORMAN
The Mystery Toss

All the hums and buzzes of where I
begin the night,
all the still and flashing little red lights
telling me I exist
in an active evening imagination
I say the ant's shadow
is beside mine.

But
I am now, will always be,
addict in the castle
during a year
when the cracks have been emptied
by a virus and lying politicians.

Such interference chasing the income
trying to be me,
none of it there when I am the witness
to winter's brief sunsets,
it is like I have taken a clock
off its boring wall,
thrown it up into air lacking snow
nobody even wants.

Aloneness the real perfection,   able to admire a dog's barking
as I pass through the path I have
not only made but tread
due to the chase I mention often
and manage despite identities
now that I ready to turn sixty-three
I seem calm about for the first time.

But
may I introduce, "Big Boy"
relaxing up the street
on his favourite lower branch.

Big Boy has brought the latest addiction--
I cannot not see him and his mate
each day along with each daughter--
one wing up and one wing down
as he caches a beak full of four peanuts
on days we know to be early Spring.

But   there's the mystery of a bed,
where does he sleep?
Where does all his family sleep?

Both questions leave me
staring at a handy puddle,
recognition of the answerless man.
How his steps adjust to the hill's ice
is only what comes first after a shift
putting up with damgerous equipment
and a supposed manager unable
to adjust his daily need to criticize
after asking a new employee to
take the initative and put away pallets,
what takes up the least amount of space.

And during the end of such a walk
toward the home he pays for
there is a stop, a place he places
a handful of dog-food, a handful
of unshelled peanuts, knowing in
the deepest parts of his body then
that there really is a soul able to
be weighted down by the walkers
he watches, and doesn't wish to be
part of, trying to get by, being other
then what can no longer not be called
what most won't say is a form of slavery.

What Big Boy sees us unable to escape,
watches me try to ask him for
any tiny bit, any type of freedom   he has, he may
drop, to be
the direction I really deserve.

But
remember, there's the bed thing.
Where would he sleep?

Frustration actually turns to wonder
as the coin's answer
finally lands in a gloveless hand
while the off-work sun arranges
a selection of white clouds,
begins to rhyme the frozen sky
with strokes of bright oranges.

ISILDA NUNES
The Dead City
Trans. from the Portuguese

in the dead city,
to the cross of indifference,
flow dreams into liquid crematoriums.
the madness decreed ride
shipwrecked desires,
on common walkways.
in the dead city,
hunger, thirst, invades hospices.
ghosts play at children
and old people get childhood.
emigrated the hugs.
there are no bridges to cross the night.
there are sales in this river,
pain on this ship.
Charon smokes a cigarette in the main ditch.
simply blackout.
simply silence.
only tomb
in the dead city.
and me?
and you?
and we?

ELIZABETH O. OGUNMODEDE
When Passion Speaks.

The demise of two friends who I would live to never forget shook me and made me bawl, all day long.

They were Karen and Carrie, two sisters who were a major part of my story. They stood by me when the world seemed to be caving in and they partook in my joy when it seemed like the doors of Heaven had opened upon me, in my favor.

I'd live to remember the lovely moments we spent together.

Thousands and thousands of luncheons we had together at pizza places, cafés, restaurants, gardens, and parks, marred and made our bond stronger.

On most evenings, we'd seat in my garden. Our picnic mat was patterned with all our favorite colors. Our picnic basket would have been filled with food, prepared by us three.

Our laughter would erupt all around the garden, as we enjoy sandwiches, fruits, bread, cakes, and juices.

Girly talks of fashion, parties and everything under the sun would never be eluded.

Then, we'd settle down with our cups of hot chocolate, read and share thoughts. It had become a tradition for us three to read the same book at the same time. Fiction and poetry were major choices.

Sometimes, Carrie would dramatize some prose work she had crafted in a falsetto voice, then, Karen would plead to read some piece of poetry I had written, out loud to nature and us in her pitchy voice.

With much confidence, she'd criticize our works. Her criticism was always sensible and full of wisdom, as a wonderful critic that she was, she was unbiased.

Some days, Karen would have some sketches which she had done to show us. Other times, she would simply sit in the peaceful garden and finish up a sketch or begin afresh, while I and Carrie made some drafts for our literary pieces.

I miss those times when we'd sit together while some sweet lyrics of great artists blended in perfect harmony with their beat and rhythm.

There were days when we'd also wander around bookstores, shopping for books, see a movie which Karen would surely criticize all day long, it was rare for my beloved friend not to find fault and errors in the plots...of books and movies, then, we'd go for a burger or small chops before heading home.

It all seems like yesterday, those times when we consoled one another and kept going, even against turbulent situations. We all repeated to one another, "when the going gets hard, the hard gets going".

We learned from each other, great principles of life that I have grown to cherish and pass on to my children.

As the years went by, I realized that I was lucky to have had friends who were as precious as gold, while growing up. Karen and Carrie were friends who worked and lived as if there is no tomorrow. They gave me their shoulders to cry on and showered me with love.

Oh! How I wish I had not invited them both to come over to that stately home in our county. I remember that it all began with a phone call.

"Why don't we meet at the stately home today instead, I'd love us to visit a greenhouse tomorrow"

And then another.

"Kelly darling, can you please come home?"

I glanced at my wristwatch, Karen and Carrie should have been here, it had been over thirty minutes since we last spoke. I'd tried calling them but neither of them was picking their calls.

"Mom," I said. "You know I should be meeting with my friends now"

I heard my mom's shaky breath and realized how unstable her voice was. "You have to come"
And then, it dawned on me, my entire body went cold.

Each time I look back at our friendship, I remember that it all ended with the beeps of the life support machines.

We all liked literature, we adored the works of men from all races of the globe. Looking back at it all, I appreciate one unique trait Karen possessed that none of us had.

I appreciate that she seemed to have the highest IQ amongst us. The way she reasoned and spoke was witty. Above all, Karen didn't write like I and her sister did, maybe, she didn't have the passion for writing but I know fervently that she was passionate when it came to highlighting errors and solving mysteries. She had always wanted to become a detective, it hurts deeply that her dream was buried with her.

Carrie, on the other hand, authored books. She and I both coauthored a few books and today when I refer to those published books I wrote with her, I can't but tell my audience of the greatest lover of literature I ever knew.

"Kids," I say to the teens around me while sipping my coffee Americano with no sugar. "You have to let the world know you exist, you have to pursue your talent, allow your passion to drive you. Never forsake your passion, what you enjoy doing is very important.

If you love art, let it be your stepping stone, science, commerce, literature, e.t.c can also be your ladder to the top if that's where your passion lies.

The nutty and earthy flavor of my coffee awakens the memory of I and Carrie, reading our favorite poem by an African poet, over cups of Americano.

'WHEN THE POETS ARE LONG GONE.
Bring back the memories of my lovely genre
It's not from the armory but from his diary
Oh! words could be more precious than big-ticket

I wondered around bookstores,
Couldn't find a copy left aside that in his diary
His lyrics were expensive
But the pen that inked them was less
The wise few couldn't help but reference his words
And men who seek knowledge, hunt for his works
Placing his diary for the print of inks, will
Bring back the value of what we seem to have lost
The gracious moment that gives me joy is knowing,
Poetic words can be immortalized, if well inked,
Let the Heavens bless the inks left behind by departed poets
©RICHARD O. OGUNMODEDE'

I paced around the room, allowing the teenagers to make notes.

Life has taught me to teach others, my audience, and readers to leave a legacy behind either written or what people will see.

RICHARD O. OGUNMODEDE
Please Don't Shade Your Love.

You picked me up from the choky garden,
Amidst thousands of beautiful and scintillating flowers,
Not minding my thorns and the color of my leaves.

You spotted the radiation that I possessed,
I was flattered by the emotions you poured,
When you perceived my scent.

You stood by me, all through the spring,
Your warm hugs saw me through the coldest winter,
You shaded me through the harsh and hot summer,

You ran your finger all through my petals,
It tickled me through the memorable fall,
That made me feel much more than a flower.

You've brought me far, to the place I least imagined,
And my beauty glows, like I'd always wished,
My soul is indebted to your caring love.

But now, I lack the ignorance,
Of what might go wrong,
While the door to your heart is almost shut.

I can imagine how you may have felt,
Journeying this far, and all the stress it took,
Nurturing me with so much love.

Could you please, re-establish your faith in me,
And watch me grow? Then see how the world,
Celebrates the beauty you have produced.

I remain the red rose, you had earlier loved,
That special rose, with much fragrance,
That had captured your heart at first glance.

TAOFEEK LÁLÉKAN ÒGÚNPÉRÍ
Justice on Trial

this moment, life screams at me
and silence tells my stories
of oppressions i cannot yet describe,
of suppressions that gag my mouth
to an audience of rainbowlike mood;
the interrogators yet steely rigid,
lance me with long looks, ready again
to quiz me, rebranding the questions
like politicians of continuity
bribing the public conscience
as they flesh an old lie
with a facade of truth; no, i say,
this is not my truth, it is ours:
young men and women, irated;
youths starved of truths so much
we have developed chronic ulcer for lies;
doctor, if you doctor me with too much
of your GMOs (Grammatically Masked Off-truths),
my hot blood, spilled as I cough to death,
will embolden the redness of your conscience.

NGOZI OLIVIA OSUOHA
Black Child

They call you coloured, as though they are colourless
And tag you awkward and still hinder your forward,
They compel you wayward and compact you untoward
Black child, the world is so wide, yet wants you wild!

The sea wants to drown you so be no fish, for fish is edible and profitable
Rather be the tide, the current and the storm
Be the mermaid, and rule the sea!

Black child, the fire wants to raze you
So be not the coal for coal is combustible,
Instead be the flame, the hotness, and the degree
Be not inflammable!

The wind wants to uproot you
Be the earth, the land and the forces!

The world doesn't like your skin
So she can throw you into the bin
Just to get the tiniest tin
Or drink the harshest gin
And still label you a sin,
If that could make her win
Or puncture you with a pin.

Black child, you are not gold
Let no one have you sold,
Though you live in a nest
You can be the best.
You are never the worst
Let no one; your head burst!

Black child, you are not a monkey
Do not be laboured like a donkey
Though you live in a cave
You are not a slave,
And never you be a pest
Though they put you to test.

Your breastmilk is sweeter than honey
Let none syphon it with money,
Your balls are stronger than rocks
Let none crush them with blocks
Nor cage them with padlocks, for there is your life!

Black child, the world is dark
But you can make a mark!
Yes, your skin is black
But there is no nature you lack!

Your skin is beautiful and wonderful
Even the rainbow is not that colourful,
Black child, walk with your shoulders high
For no human is more human than you!

FRANCIS OTOLE
Still I Rise

thrown overboard into the Atlantic,
meal for the aquatic.
a buoy; still I rise.

ripped from solace,
cast into furnace.
a gold; still I rise.

stripped of ego
to hide like gecko.
a star; still I rise.

flushed down history
to wallow in misery.
a diamond; still I rise.

grounded to dust,
left to rust.
a pyramid; still I rise.

thrown into flame
to be consumed by shame.
a Phoenix; I still rise.

cut to pieces
never to find where peace is.
A hydra; still I rise.

born of resilience
nurtured by pestilence.
An African; I still rise.

CARLO PARCELLI
The Love Song of Jay Vivian Chambers
(aka Whittaker Chambers)

I want to fuck you Alger Hiss;
Hoover your almost Plymouth rocks
And with my face between your Harvard hips
Fix my mordant mouth
About your commie Brahman cock.
My polecat prick poking about your anus
Jousting with Ate at your embargoed hole
Who among these hypocrites
And liars dare blame us,
A Democrat and a Republican
Passionately soiled as one Hegelian soul?
Draped in our red, white, black and blue
What other pumpkin could both
So perfectly love you and yet be a mole
Whose very being abjures the truth?
Let Angleton and Dulles have their skullduggery
As in the gloved hands of Calvinist whores
They secrete the bugs that tattle our buggery
And love becomes the cold weapon of war.
Let Cohn have his golden boy
And "Tail-Gunner" Joe his hotel prats
While James Jesus Angleton looks
     Down upon them all
Concealed behind the closet slats.

Alger, I would strap you to a chair and
The garters from your argyle socks unloose.
As I stir you with a French Judas kiss
And recruit your necktie as a noose.
And between the turmoil of Lutheran loathing
     And pagan need
   Stab you in your back-
     Side until you bleed,
Loving you to death in my serpent's embrace
And plead the 'good' people not be called upon
   To decide our case.

What is the tide but salt cycling in a wounded moon,
Like petty gods we have caballed stars
 That ran with rivers of alien blood,
   And insisted they had been rendered ours.
Here, we find the corpse of Baudelaire on Mars;
   There is nothing left to disbelieve.

Every lie has succeeded repeatedly
And every soul habitually deceived
    As death brings victims sweet relief
And truth is but another invitation to grieve.

MONALISA PARIDA
Metamorphosis

There was a girl
Who lived in a querencia
A secret garden,
Where love, light surrounds.
Enchantress soul uses passionate fire.
When a moment changed
Everything in her life.
Now,
She is getting fear
More than yesterday.
If She goes back to her safe place alone........
Would the sea notice her absence.
Recognise the emptiness
And the calmer waves to her children?
One day,
She will look back for him
And she will she him again.

EVA PETROPOYLOU LIANOU
To the unknown man

Long distance relationship

Days you smile
Nights I cry
Days u become silent
I become so communicative

Birds are coming from far lands
Back to their nest
Wondering will you come to our nest
Long distance relationship
My why become so long
Your words are a rainbow
In my rainy moments

Hope the heaven hear my prayers
Soon you are free from unknown chains

Hear my heart beat
Hear my heart voice

More and more
Every day
Every night
Singing for you
My precious man...

CLAUDIA PICCINNO
In the alphanumeric code

You didn't know you were
in the alphanumeric code
of my every access.
Dates, anniversaries, memories
difficult to decipher.
How anonymous is your face
behind a screen.
Quiet is the glitter
of the look.
Extinguished is my smile
of circumstance.
I receive every day
love letters
poems that swell
the book of flatterers.
I read them without surprise,
I catalog them in a protocol
which looks like a reptile house.
I prepare myself for silence.
My mind is looking for coolness
of an Augustan night and
everything else is noise.

JONATHAN RIZZO
Children and Small Fish

I like fairy tales.
But not those with Princes and Princesses,
royal weddings and royal babies attached,
that I don't care about
and in truth I find sad and empty of colors, magic and humanity
in their pompous military and imperial parade.
Crowned heads adorned with rotting shells.
The only fairy tales worth writing
and that I want to read to my children
they are of children like them who cross the sea.
They set sail, sail, dock and grow.
Of children who become men.
Of children who become princes.
Of children who marry Princesses.
Of children marrying girls
that cross the sea to become
Princesses bringing rare beauties in dowry,
solar ray of distant oases.
Children, little Princes and brave sailors.
Beautiful fairy tales
where you can close
with a happy ending,
gentle limit, border coast,
the beginning of the journey its first end.
As in the Mediterranean,
western gate and tombstone
of our Christian morality.
Here it lies and sinks
what remains of our humanity.
Floats like wood on a cross,
tsunami of compassion
that brings little fish back to shreds on the beach.
The little fish children,
dancing confetti,
free roundabouts,
the butterflies of the deep sea.
Ulysses, an old man with a weary beard,
stubborn memory,
remained on the sea to watch
the distant stars
in their eternal chatter they dance,
caresses, shores, shore, eternal wandering, just sailing, the stars, the sea.
The silence the waves returned.
The mirror of "Nobody" reflected back.

Odysseus Mediterranean meat
to count
on the sand the bone
subtract.
Ports closed for offended castaways.
Sailors,
no man abandons himself into the sea.
At the cost of not returning
with him,
at cost.
While Ulysses on his knees
he held the dirt in his hands,
little fishes in love kissed his feet,
like blossoming hedgehog flowers
and thorn petals in the eye,
Ulysses the sailor, Ulysses the castaway.
Beautiful fairy tales
when it's not raining,
read like clouds.

LAVAN ROBINSON
Rise

The character of a person soul is more important than a reputation. You cannot hide your character as it becomes visibly known to others. You also can't replace it with another. It'll ride and die with you. It can lead to a life of pleasure, happiness, and blessings or to a road of misery, grief, and doom. You build reputation through numerous feats in your journey of life. Your character is validated through what lies deep inside. What separates them both is a very thin line and this one thing you definitely have to keep in mind. Materialistic bling can only temporarily disguise from the outside. It's when trouble, storms and adversity comes that one's true character will either to the challenge quiver, fall and run away or step up to it and triumphantly rise.

AMITA SANGHAVI
'Being rich'

Rich as in
Thought,
Word,
Deed,
Values.

Rich as in
Not indebted

Rich as in
Having
A
Child

Rich as in
Having a home
In each friend's house

Rich as in
Having a smile
And
Simultaneous tears

Rich as in
Having
More than enough
To spend
And enough to spare
For a needy

Rich as in
Having a home
Filled with
Colors
And coffee stains.

Rich in pain,
And therefore
Richer in forgiveness,
And rich in
Mindfulness of trying
Not to hurt another.

Rich in love
From a little doggie
And a pretty, tall daughter.

Yes, rich in faith
Extraordinarily rich,
In the knowledge
That miracles happen.

And richest
To have you
As a divine creation
In my life!

SANKHA SEN
When I met Me

We just finished our desert after supper. It's been a habit to go to our gardens and take a stroll before I go to bed. Watching the stars, instigating my quest to know me. Who am I? How do people perceive me from outside? Why am I a boy? What happens if I were born a girl? What is within my consciousness?

When such thoughts were trying to find its places within my neurons, the clouds faded away and the the clear sky became visible. The bright shining moon showing up a hope of finding answers to all such questions. And I heard a familiar female voice from our house within.

"Milan, it's time to go to bed," Mom called onto me.

I reluctantly came to my bedroom, sorted out my books, lying hay while on my bed. Books like "The Parallel Universe", "The theory of relativity", "A brief History of time", "Awakening beyond Non-Duality" and many more have become part of my thinking and living process.

A gust of wind from the window attracted my attention and called me to the fascinating universe, as probably the same wind had been successful in clearing the sky once again and gifted me with the view of the magnificence. Perplexed with its enormity and lost in its artistic endurance, classified, and categorized my existence limited by countable power of my senses. I can imagine me slipping into a transitional state from wakefulness onto the onset of sleep.

A mild light woke me up, strangely the light of this sun appeared quite mild. I went up to the oval shaped window to see the outside world which is normally my habit. Every morning I rather try to identify my identity. No birds on the trees, wait a moment, these are not trees, somewhat like branches with full of flowers but no leaves. I could still relate myself in this new dawn. Someone banged on the door, voice appeared familiar, its mom,

"Milan, it's time for the college, come have your breakfast," mom called.

I brushed my teeth and climbed down the stairs. Mom cooked beacons and Omelette for breakfast.

"Mom, did I sleep a little longer," I asked.

"Yes, you did," Dad answered.

Felt secured with the answer from my dad.

Rushed up to my room. Tried to get hold of my books, but where are all my books. What I found were some gadgets and some hard copies of e-books. I could relate the gadgets to the Touch Pads which I knew.

Went out of our house, was stunned to have a clear view of the sky. How come so many planets were visible? At least there were two Black holes which were within visible range.

I asked my dad, "In which Galaxy are we in?"

He said," It's called Galaxy Alpha; we had travelled from our very own Milky way galaxy almost a decade ago through the wormhole and landed at this end of the Black hole. We have reached a parallel universe and found ourselves here."

Obviously, a question popped up. "Did you find your replica in this Universe," I added.

"No, not yet I even didn't make any effort to find him," said dad.

Just imagine a worm digging the apple from one end to another; similarly, from the concept of Einstein's theory of general relativity comes this concept that such wormholes might connect two parallel universes and we might as well be able to travel between universes.

String theory is another interesting theory in which we might find that our universe is not only one, but other universes also exist. This might lead us to theoretize that as there could be a copy of me sitting in one universe perceiving and acting in a way while simultaneously there might be another copy of me perceiving and acting in another way in a parallel universe.

Time travel, if it may be possible, might lead to interesting Paradoxes, one of them is named as Grandfather Paradox, where a person time travelling and reaching it past, kills his own grandfather, might lead to a very big question on his own birth and identity.

People sometime think that the things which we see around us could be a mental representation of the things perceived by our mind, which can be totally different to what which we actually perceive. The mind could be the centre of universe, which is relative to the point of reference. Wherever we go, the point of reference moves with us, so in that way the centre of universe can be all over.

I asked my dad, "How did we land up to this world?"

He said, "Do you realize in which we are now?"

I said, "No books but only gadgets. Definitely we are in a different world but know nothing more."

My Dad added "We are now in the 20300-calendar year, comparable to our world. Although they have a different way of calculating. For them it is 120300, as they have different historical point of start. They knew everything about our world, so people of these universe informed me in which year we are now in. We had the possibility to travel space and time through the wormhole and finally we landed up in this parallel universe."

"So, Dad do I get to meet my copy in this Universe," I added.

"Theoretically yes, but don't know where he or she might be now," my dad answered.

"Why are you saying he or she?" I added.

"Didn't you realize by now, in this world, changing gender is a regular thing. So, who knows in which gender your replica has chosen to stay in this universe," Dad explained.

"What about consciousness and thinking pattern, does that change too?" I curiously asked.
"I do not have an answer to that, if by chance you get to meet your copy do find that out. By the way I need to go now, have a great day", Dad concluded the conversation as he was in a rush.

I too packed my gadgets and went on to my college. In the break I happened to sneak into the e-library. Was just scanning through Literature section. Then an e-book came into my notice. The title was quite fascinating *'When I met Me'* by Gabriela Brown.

Somehow this e-book just pulled me in, and I downloaded it and requested online a hard copy out of it. There was a choice, we could either read the book as soft copy, which might cost a nominal amount but if we ordered for a hard copy, it might cost somewhat more. Don't know why I still feel comfortable reading hard copies. May be my eyes are more comfortable with printed Literature.

In this Universe it's not that different to what we do in our universe. Good to know that Literature in both the Universes still occupy the hearts of so many readers.

As I received the hard copies of the book within a day, I planned to read the book in the weekends.

I searched for Gabriela Brown, found her whereabouts. She was a scientist and a writer.
It was Friday and drizzling very much. My school was over. My eyes went towards the Book. Just made me a tea and lied on the bed and started reading the book.

It talked about many fascinating things. She was also searching some answers, which came out quite clearly in her writing. Search for her identity, search for her feelings as a lady. She tried to bring in a way how she can get a command over her hormones and how can she think like a male person even being a female. How can she come out of her existence and experience herself as an outsider? It did not sound like multiple personality disorder. What she was trying to tell was, how can she come out of the limits of her brains ability to think just like a woman herself.
Something interested me very much. She was trying to understand why her brain thinks that way. On what all factors does her thinking and choices depend. And on the same issue does another being think differently. The involuntary misalignment in thoughts of varied individuals was something she was trying to confront.

Why does people's choices differ in logic, emotion, guilty feelings, morality? Things appearing true to someone may appear untrue to others. Why does our mind gets attracted to something even though our sense of morality tells to subdue such desires.

The restriction to one's impulse is what humans practice to become more human in his or her manners. The quest to adapt to circumstantial situations is a debatable issue. A man or a woman is born, learns to shape up to fit in the flow and then raises the next generation to keep up the genetic immortality alive. And then dies, hoping that something might continue to exist. If we live in our present without thinking what might just happen tomorrow, we somehow take a resort to a temporary happiness. And that's what human's main attractions are: Happiness and pleasure. Different people seek happiness in different ways. Considering the socio-economic balance, humans have developed statistics in which he or she can turn the life plan into a predictable journey, whose timetables are quite a routine. Facing challenges is something which does keep humans catch up to the speed of evolution.

The more I was reading, the more I felt similarity in her thoughts. There had been lots of questions which find its place in this book. I started to check on her whereabouts again.
As I found, she was a scientist working in Medical Research where Hormone therapy happened, and we know that Estrogen Hormone Therapy possibly allows a transition from a male to a female.

I did get in touch with the publisher and got her contact details. The publishers were reluctant in providing me her contact details, but after signing a confidentiality agreement, I was provided her contact details.

What is it that keeps us motivated to go into unknown territories? The Mind and Heart tries to compromise its dissimilarities. Is the real happiness found in a proper handshake of mind and the heart? These are some of the questions which kept me moving towards Gabriela.

In the meantime, in the News, it was shown that there had been some problem in the inter-universe travels as people could not successfully reach another Universe through wormholes. Many people were lost trying to travel to their desired universes and no whereabouts have been recorded yet.

I see certain challenges in multiverse travels because a stable communication is required to be im-proved. The genetic identity is also somewhat I haven't really heard of. Meaning, if we have a person in two different universes, is there a way to keep a track of this? Did learn about Genetic lineages, which might target continuing mutations to meet its ancestral genetic variant. Now the question is, does changing one's gender or figuring out one's lineage destination across universes, guarantee in which stage of intelligence evolution are we located?

She stayed somewhere in the same city. Only thing was, I needed to discuss this with my parents.
After sipping the appetizer, chicken soup, I took the chance to explain my situation.

"Dad and Mom, this weekend I would try to get in touch with Gabriela, as after reading her book I could identify my inner being. Many questions did knock the unconscious door to my deeper identity. Clueless about whom I am yet to meet, I am feeling a call of my own being.," I explained.

Dad said, "How did you get her book?"

I said I was just scrolling the books and the title of the book really fascinated me.

"How can we help you," Mom added.

"Mom and dad, if you both want to join me, you all are most welcome," I insisted.

Somehow my dad and mom took lot more interest in the topic and my dad said, "Can you share the book; we would like to have a look at the same."

It was a Friday morning; the scrambled eggs were ready.

Mom asked, "Do you need the extra bit of cheese?"

I said, "Off course, it's the right age to consume lactic delicacies."

By the way, I really love cheese a lot and mom knew that.

"I really glanced through your book, and surprisingly I am too keen to meet the author. Really want to understand her thoughts and frankly speaking, I am too quiet familiar with many such ideas," my dad started to explain.

Mom too added, "I didn't have much time to read the book as it was mostly with your dad. But still I did sneak a bit and loved some portions which I managed to read in between running daily errands."

I was curious that night and really got hold of the book and rechecked those portions which mostly interested me.

I woke up with a sound of the main door opening. Heard the faint voice of my dad,

"Come down you two, we should leave in 30 minutes."

We were all set to go.

"Did you call her and inform that we are coming," my dad instigated.

"Yes, I did inform her, she was little surprised. I explained her the reason, she was initially reluctant but finally agreed," I answered.

The doorbell rang and a voice came from the speaker, and Gabriela saw us and let us in. She told us to wait in the drawing room. We were looking at her digital 3D photos. Her room does speak a lot about her insights.

"Hello, there," came a voice. I turned around to see a reflection of me in this feminine character.

"I am really glad to know that at least someone did like my book and came all the way to meet me. I am really honoured," she said.

She offered us some snacks and asked us to tell, what is that we want to know. Her looks, height and posture were very similar to mine. Her living room had a mix of feminine and masculine deco items.

"Do you belong to this Universe?" I straight came to the point.

She was a bit surprised but said "What really makes you think that way?" she said.

Then I explained that we came from a different universe and landed up here.

"I too don't belong here," said she.

"By the way I did a gender transformation and originally I was a man," she surprised us all.

"I wanted to feel like a woman and correlate the same with a man's thinking," she added.

"As you might have known from my writings that I am interested in lineage mappings for example something like the grandfather conflict. I have access to a software which can map back and identify our pedigree and origin," she continued.

I was curious to know about my identity. "Can we check our origin?" I reinstated.

"Sure, do come to my domestic Lab," she invited us.

It was a glass room full of touch screen monitors. She touched one button which scanned her body and then opened a software.

"Please go there and stand on that spot, the scanner needs to scan you," she explained.

I did, it took almost 15 minutes to finish the scan. The screen showed the lineage of my pedigree.

She surprising shouted "Oh my God!"

We were all surprised and asked, "What happened?"

She rushed to another screen and pressed her thumb and then popped up her own lineage path. Then she dragged and dropped hers over mine.

"Look at this if you see this branch, it coincides here," she tried to explain.

I said, "Does that mean we are the same person having the same origin but have grown differently in two parallel universes?"

"Exactly," she kept on staring at me for some minutes.

"I see myself in you and vice versa," I added.

My parents were stunt with this conclusion.

"What a great coincidence, we are the same person undergoing two different evolutions in two different universes. I underwent a gender transformation, so I am the feminine part of you," she said, and her eyes was glaring.

Dad said, "This means we could also be the replicas of your parents."

"Logically possible," said Gabriela.

Dad worked in a Television Channel.

He insisted, "Our TV Channel would be glad to host a public interview session with both of you live on Sunday."

Gabriela was out of words; she could not express her feelings as she took some time to digest this situation. She just rushed out of the Lab and went to the Lawn to breathe in some fresh air.

We followed her and asked her gently, "Are you okay? Do you need to drink a glass of water?"

She just watched the stars and said, "Yes this is unique, and the world should know about it, yes I would do the interview."

The camera man indicated to us, "1 2 3 Start Rolling!"

"Good evening, ladies and gentlemen here I am taking the pleasure in introducing Gabriela Brown who is none other than me. Ladies and Gentlemen, yes, she is a copy of mine from a parallel universe and she has undergone gender transformation and now he is a she. So, you all see me in two forms, one as a man that's me and one as a woman, that's her," I started the introduction part.

There was a huge cheer amongst the audience in the TV Studio. People were allowed to ask questions.

"Do you get a feeling of belonging to your own copy? What has actually pulled you both together?" one person from the audience questioned.

"What are you? Siblings or something else?" another person from the audience added.

"Great question, what has pulled me was her writing. Her writing had brought out many topics which I thought of too. That really explains why there were so many similarities between both of us. I felt I somehow belong to these thoughts," I answered.

Gabriela answered, "We are the same person, can't call us siblings. We can see ourselves as each other's reflection."

"As you both appear to be the same person but are opposite in genders, how do both of you perceive the situations differently?" questioned another person from the audience.

I answered, "It's a good question, I guess Gabriela can answer this better, because she has gone through both perspectives."

"Since I have gone through both the traits, I can somewhat judge myself being on either side of the gender. It is true that men and women might excel in different forms of assignments. The brain might categorize the different cognitive and behavioral aspects differently. The physical limitations or advantages does lead to certain misunderstandings. But the intentions merge into a common success point. The gender thoughts kind of compliment in each other. The emotional and the intellectual aspects does complete the circle. May be that's why the continuity of the generations does remain in the success of the perfect match which is nothing but an amazing wonder of the Nature. But above all the mental compatibility drives eventually to the longevity of any relation," Gabriella concluded.

"How do you both perceive each other?" questioned another person.

I replied to him by reciting this poem written by me,

"May you all be the blessed choice of the Unknown.
May you all be mere existence without bonds of time and space.
There exists a way to perceive a woman with a man's heart…
Tearing one out of its own…
To be drowned within self reflection…
Adoring the magnificence of the Creator…
Multiverses, Multi-dimensions, may not defer the Truth far away…

Who's within who's not within lost may be me in unconscious consciousness.
The vastness of the Explore burning within ignorance.
The more we sync the more I adore…
I meet me in space and time, what in a life can I ask for more!"

The audience broke out clapping and applauding.

Gabriela looked at me, smiled and said "Brilliant, let us start to know us with each other's inquisitiveness."

I hear someone removing the curtains very hard, and suddenly a flash of sunlight hit my eyes and I woke up.

I cried "Oh no!"

"What happened, come wake up, the breakfast is ready," that's the same old familiar voice of my mom.

Yes, I returned to my own Universe!

originally published in the book "Collection of Feelings" published by Haoajan in Kolkata, India. Reviewed and modified a bit by the author afterwards.

TALI COHEN SHABBTAI
I Am Tali

I read prose only in the third person,
and only translated prose,
poetry, I also read in Hebrew.

I love Wislawa Szymborska, she copies in written word
the creation
in a brilliant fashion, and was recognized during her lifetime and was not among
the female poets who danced the 'dance of death in life'
for that I lowered her credit.

I think it's impossible to tag in one breath! A contemporary poetess with
characters that preserved the myth of the 'cursed poetesses'. For they are
found only in the underground or tomb
There is no negotiation with this judgement

Mainstreamism repels me.
Bestsellers I do not touch.
I love nonfiction books.
Newspapers do not count at all as the writing and reading genre.

And my therapist I address in the second person singular
while omitting the third degree: "doctor", it's ok, it's acceptable –
many poetesses have sat in my chair in front of him
Anne Sexton, Sylvia Plath,
and those who ended up as their own hangman.

I often write in the first person singular and also to talk
It is
my way to circumvent
myself from afar.

And do not ask what I often write about! I do not like rhetorical questions that belittle
my intellect.
Tali Cohen Shabtai.

ROBERT SIMON
Friday Night in Kennesaw

From thirty rows up I could see
The whole of the field, spread out
Its former farmland made spritely for
Visitors, players, instrumentalists mulling about

While the local team hammered the opposition,
They call them warriors for days like this
When nothing but lines of teenagers
And aggression can't be sealed with a kiss

Or parents observing above. The stands,
Metal antiquities pressed to hard, durable seating
From forges and the 200-decibel loudspeaker to my right,
And to my left, the mother I met at meet and greet

Two years ago, dancing to the kickoff chant,
A reminder of 90s clubs and flip phones we left behind
Along with follicles and long dried conditioner,
Of which those on the field have no knowledge,

Nor would the child, holding her euphonium, marching
For the first time across that same field, smile intact,
And her father, iPhone raised in solemn recording,
While the lady to my side tells me about why she's apt

To go back to school after four kids and twenty years
Of no job, loudspeaker still pushing us against our hands
And breezes, not from voice or line or even musical chants,
Can take us back onto the lost and ever clamoring lands.

ANANTA KUMAR SINGH
A Little Drop of Water

A little drop of water
Evoke imagine of the creatures
A little drop of water
Refresh trees branches
A little drop of water
The Elegant Beauty of the nature
A little drop of water
Splendour blooms of the flowers
A little drop of water
Express the feelings of the writers
A little drop of water
Monsoon is the season of love.

PANKHURI SINHA
The politics of re-starting

The politics of re-starting
Rather the conditions of it
Because
No one should have to re-start like this
The study
They have dreamt of
All their lives
Their great big research project
Made up of digging into the archives
And the books before that
The lovely, outwordly books
From the library
With the hard cover
The old ones
Looking sacred almost
But may be
Not so lovely
As you read between the arguments
And get to the settling of finances
In all colonial history
But not even being able to focus on that
No one should have to re-start like this
Calling attorneys
At home
Sending details of robbed rights
In a hasty, shocking divorce
Details going back into the years
Of how and when you first
Met your husband
Details that included all of our ancestry
Involving even our grandfathers
Grandmothers
Long, lost relations
All the office corruption
And ways of dealing with it.
Calling attorneys in different places
And finding out about one's stolen rights
While working with a similar set of people
Is an extremely toll taking way of re-starting
Simply letting go
Forgetting your pain
While being in it
Is impossible.
And there cannot be a conference

Debating the best way of cure
All they debate, dissect, is your life
They increase pain
They increase problems
There can be no conference
Looking for cure
Unless it is a law conference
Discussing
How best to punish the offenders.
Conferences
Have a history
Of inflicting brutal talk on me.

HOWARD STEIN
In the Neighborhood
"Good fences make good neighbors."   Robert Frost

In the neighborhood,
Houses, garages, cars,
Post oak, scrub oak, blackjack,
Occupy both sides of a narrow road –
The same species of trees,
An extended family,
Related by roots and acorns,
And in autumn, high waves
Of fallen leaves.

Our human neighbors are friendly,
Ready to help in some mishap –
But nonetheless distinguish "my trees"
From "your trees" – we all
Know the distinction.
Still, we call ourselves
A neighborhood;
The road is passageway
To get around in our community.

Squirrels and birds say otherwise;
Squirrels scurry across the inconvenience
As if they owned the place –
"These are all *our* trees,
What matter *your* road to us?"
Birds, equally oblivious
To our boundaries and streets,
Fly, land, nest, raise families
In whose ever yard they choose –
Though they, too, have
Their own rules of spacing.

I cast my lot
With birds and squirrels,
And with their trees,
Who visit across the fences
We build to separate
Our real estate from our neighbors'.
Whatever our next barrier,
They will outwit
Our every property line
And zoning law –

What we build
They will defy,
So long as this earth
Shall live.

PAUL STROBLE
Psalm in Snow

Deep snowfall, ten degrees.
Our pastor isn't sure
whether to cancel church or not.

We're not sure, either,
no one is, but our neighbor lady
lives for the House of the Lord.

Snow stacks upon the fields of those
who have walked through valleys of shadows,
and Pastor shepherds them.

She perfects her sermon
on goodness and mercy, watches, prays,
makes a snowman with the youth.

Afternoon turns to evening,
the early moonlight is a voice
that is not heard but heard everywhere,

like the calm of the stars,
the timber of the county, hills
and ravines arrayed more than Solomon.

God asks, have you visited
the storehouses of snow,
can you loosen the cords of Orion?

We make angels in white, loved by the one
from whom comes the hoar-frost of heaven,
channels of snow, Christ in cold.

Folks and Pastor phone: let's try to meet.
You know Miss Audie will come anyway,
and what is snow but still waters?

First published in Paul Stroble, Small Corner of the Stars (Georgetown, KY: Finishing Line Press, 2017) 34.

SUSHANT THAPA
Bearings

Give me words
I will make connotative out of it.
Give me denotative, I shall mean what I seek.
I have molten and liquified assurances;
From my ageless saints who were
Proponents of figurative languages.
Human departures speak how the night cries.
Left in a tranquility I wake up
From the termites infested bed;
The wood also rots in the
Forgetful dream-work.
Like my resting backbone, the wordsmith
Is straightening the minuteness in my belief.
Everyone is a victim of rain;
Unless shelter is provided.
Fragments also mean
The same in wholeness.
There is a desire for new color
To paint the nuances of life.
Old is still a color of the bearings
That recall the timelessness.

JERENA TOBIASEN
Best Friends

The young girl stood at the edge of the forest. It was late, the dark night lit only by a sliver of moon. Behind her, she heard her parents calling, pleading for her to return. She knew that would never happen. Her determination kept her feet facing forward, despite a slight sway to the contrary.

"Julia!" Their mingled voices drifted on the evening dew. "Julia, come back, dear. We love you."

"No," Julia said with quiet determination. "I must go, no matter what."

A deep woof announced the rival of her best friend Pal, a black Labrador Retriever. On her second birthday, Julia's father had placed the small puppy in her arms and made her promise to love and care for him, or he would give the puppy to someone else. Determined to keep her promise, the young girl nodded ferociously, clutching the puppy to her chest as he squirmed to be released.

Julia had kept her promise. For ten years, she had ensured that Pal was fed, groomed, walked and taken to the veterinarian for regular check-ups. Until he understood his responsibility as Julia's companion, he was placed in a pen next to Julia's bed at night, and only allowed to roam during the day. Once he understood that he should use a corner at the back of the yard for his business, and that he should ask to be let out to do so, Pal was allowed to sleep at the foot of her bed.

Julia's mother tucked her into bed each night, caressing her hair and kissing her forehead. Then she pet Pal's head and called him 'good dog' before she turned out the light and closed the door. As soon as Pal heard the latch catch, he crawled on his belly until he stretched beside his best friend, his head resting on the pillow next to hers.

Pal matured faster than Julia and, by the time she was ready to start school, he had become her protector. Each school day, they set off together, meeting up with Julia's friends along the way. When the school bell rang, Julia would tell Pal to go home and come back later. Pal did as he was told.

This evening, Julia had said goodbye to Pal. She knew he could not accompany her through the forest. Surprised to hear his approach, she bent down and hugged his neck, rubbing her cheek against his glossy, black coat.

"Pal," she said scolding the dog, "I told you not to come."

Julia could not be mad at her friend. She loved him too much. Instead, she scrubbed behind his ears, and giggled when he licked her nose.

"Don't say I didn't warn you," Julia said. "The forest can be spooky at night."

An owl hooted in the old oak tree towering above them, startling Julia.

"Come on," Julia said. "We may as well get this over with." She glanced at her friend, wrapping her fingers around his collar for confidence. "I'm glad you came."

Together, the dog and the young girl stepped onto the narrow path that led into the forest. The owl hooted again, as if to warn them. They had not walked far when something scooted across their path squeaking. Julia gasped. As if sensing her fear, Pal woofed again and licked her arm before stepping forward. Still holding his collar, Julia followed.

Quiet settled around them as Julia's eyes and ears adapted to the darkness. She inhaled the damp, mossy odour of ancient rot and felt a calm blanket her.

"I never realized how loud the forest can be at night," she said, not expecting a reply. "It's not quiet in here at all. Listen!"

They took tentative steps into the dark, listening to chirping laments, scurrying feet, owl hoots. *Snap!* Julia jumped at the sound of the breaking twig.

"What was that?" She listened again, squinting into the dark. Pal tugged her along the path. *Snap!*

"Woof!" Pal barked with authority, his long tongue bobbing in and out of his open mouth. "Woof!"

Julia stiffened with fear when the dog stopped abruptly, lowering his head and growling. High above the treetops, a cloud shifted, exposing the sliver moon to cast light on the path. Masked white faces of a mother racoon and three babies shaped like teapots glowed in the luminescence.

"Woof!" Pal barked again, as if to scold the racoons for scaring them. Seeming embarrassed, the racoons disappeared hastily into the brush. Pal pulled again.

The sounds of the forest grew louder as Julia and Pal approached its far side. Songbirds seemed to sing with joy, the owl's hoots marking the low notes, the forest susurration filling in a soothing background.

"How curious?" Julia said. "The night has only fallen, yet I see sunlight ahead. Surely we cannot have been in the forest for so long."

Pal sneezed and shook his head, love reflecting in his gleaming eyes. He rested his head against her thigh.

"Thank you, Pal," Julia said, bending to hug his neck again. "As always, you have seen me safely along the path, but I think you should return home to mother and father. They will need you to comfort them when they realize I won't return. I must walk free of the forest myself." She allowed him to wash her face with his loving licks, then rubbed her cheeks dry on his glossy coat. "Go now," she said in a whisper, and watched as he raced back along the path, his tail wagging happily from side to side.

Julia stood tall, straightened her nightgown and tossed golden waves over her shoulder. Taking a deep breath, she steeled herself and stepped free of the forest into the blinding light.

"Hello, Julia," a kindly voice said. "We've been waiting for you. Welcome."

~

"Woof! Woof!" Pal barked as he approached the back door of the home that he had shared with Julia for the past ten years. "Woof! Woof!"

"Pal!" Julia's father said, opening the door. "You've missed her, old friend, but I'm sure she'd be happy to know you're safe."

Pal raced passed Julia's father, tripping up the stairs to her bedroom. Julia's mother sat quietly in an old green chair next to Julia's bed, tears staining her pale cheeks. He licked her hand, turned to the bed and jumped. Instead of resting at the foot of the bed as he always did, he dropped gently beside his best friend, resting his head on the pillow next to hers, her eyes closed in perpetual sleep.

"Good dog," Julia's mother said.

JERENA TOBIASEN
The Gardener's Mistress

Engaged as a sub-gardener at the age of fourteen, Victor Fife had worked his entire life in servitude to the estate of the late Earl of Carrick. After eighty-six years, he stood alone in the empty greenhouse attached to the garden in which the castle's vegetables and herbs had been grown. Empty but for one ancient plant imported from the Americas a month before it had been assigned to him as its sole caregiver. It was so small that the pot in which it had been rooted fit snuggly in his young hands.

Through rheumy eyes, Victor scanned the empty greenhouse remembering the grandeur first revealed to him – a myriad of exotic flora bearing unique blossoms and fruit, like banana vines, tomato plants, pawpaw trees, cucumbers, pumpkins and other gourd vines, the beauty and marvel of which he could never have imagined, but for his fortunate employment. Some plants did not bear fruit. Instead, they bore beautiful, often fragrant and always colourful blooms, including small monkey-face orchids from Peru and the putrid smelling plant nicknamed the *Corpse. Fortunately,* he thought, *that one had rarely bloomed.*

With trembling hands, he raised a cup as small as the pot with which he had first been blessed and drank deeply of the clear, tasteless liquid.

It was the Earl's wife who had driven the acquisition of the unusual plants - her preferred pastime. She had borne the Earl the required number of children then abandoned them to the care of a nursemaid. She had refused any form of needle work, or other tasks expected of genteel women. Victor Fife had often overheard her muttering that gardening was her passion. *Indeed,* he thought, *that passion had been obvious.*

On the occasion of each new acquisition for her greenhouse, the Lady of Carrick had engaged a child from the village as its caregiver. Each engagement had been for the lifetime of the plant, thereby ensuring guaranteed employment so long as the child took care to be successful. Some children had lasted only a matter of weeks or months, forced to return to their families in tears and shame for having caused the demise of one of the estate's priceless plants.

I won't be one to return in tears, Victor had declared confidently, as he had set off all those years before, and, indeed, he had not. After eighty-six years, he had outlived them all . . . even the lady who had acquired *his* curious plant and engaged him as its tender.

Victor sighed and stroked the edge of a silky bloom affectionately. "I have lived a hundred years," he said hoarsely. "My bones creak, my plumbing is faulty, my teeth have rotted. It won't be long before my beating heart ceases. Then what shall become of you my love?" His trembling hand reached to stroke another bloom.

Tears escaped his near-blind eyes. He felt the need for sleep overwhelm him.

"We are both old, my friend," he said wearily. "And we have lived well. You have grown in size and stature all these years, because I have loved and tended you well. So well, that you shall outlive me only for a short time. Alas, this one last meal will be the death of you too."

With that final statement, Victor shed his clothes and climbed onto the cushiony pillows of his beloved bloom. His devotion had cost him both wife and family, but his pride had brought the estate honours and awards beyond anything his employer had ever imagined.

He tickled the fringe of hairs as delicate as eye lashes and felt the cushions rise to embrace him. He tickled them again and felt the gentle pressure cocoon him as a lover never had. He wriggled a few more times, seeking a comfortable position. As his mind drifted on the opium cloud, he felt his lover's sticky juices squirt over him like saliva. *Soon,* he thought, *soon, you shall release me of my obligations and my loneliness. Soon…*

~

Some weeks later, a gardener from a neighbouring estate opened the greenhouse door calling Victor Fife's name. When Victor failed to answer, the neighbour stepped into the massive, empty building that had once seen such splendor, only to find the old man's prized Venus Flytrap in its last throes of death. Next to it sat a neat pile of Victor's clothing.

J R TUREK
Pillow Moon Over a Night Drive

cruising to the serene sounds of poetry on cd
liquid silvered streams caught
in headlight beams drive dark shadows away
fill my head with crystal images
that sing as I caress the rim of the wheel,
satiate my craving for down-filled solace,
for companionship for easing a long drive,
twitching my hands with the want
to write like him, to get inside his head,
to know what he knows,
to lie prone beside him
as he reads his dreams to me –
it's the floetry of it all

smooth lines paused for impact
like steady white lines beside my tires
language rolling on like the miles, draining
my mind of baggage, opening lanes to journey
where he wills me to go, hand held in his
immersed in floetry

too soon I reach my destination
still he speaks to me of his love for poetry
shows me the view from his window
has me tasting sweet tangerines
juice pooling at the corners of my mouth,
smelling onion grass in a fresh-cut field
or are they my poems flowing
through his, through me –
I rush through my assignation,
start the cd for the languid drive home
he climbs in beside me,
our time together to share secrets,
to float in my love of his floetry

Previously published in Midnight on the Eve of Never, J R Turek; Words With Wings Press; 2019

CHIKA UDEKWE
The Flame

I have seen fires in their desirable strength to burn to ashes the hearts of men. I have in a little period felt the heat of their closeness to my young soul; it was rarely warm and satisfying. But none has flame. And this, as I have convinced myself though not absolutely, makes me ignore these fires most times. My mind one February evening uttered audibly that any lady that should be a fire or created as one or seen with such magnificent beauty of fire should have a flame. Fire has a long tongue. Though not as soft and steadily watery as ours, and not in any way brief as ours too. It is this tongue that touches sincerely every heart of a noble man and the holy heaven. The truth in this be that the fire's beauty is its strength and its strength its vigorous flame. And so the lady's beauty is her character and her character her true love.

UCHE FRANCIS UWADINACHI
A New Beginning

Let me love you
by the moonsong candles
unminding the threat
of the queen's eclipse
Kissing you by the fires
of the first fireflies
with the saints and stars
keeping delightful vigil
hoping to rise anew
to the rays of morning
of a new beginning
in your warm embrace.

AMRITA VALAN
The Proposal

He sat me down on a plush sofa couch
In an elegant nook,
A stately French window did it overlook
And from the corner of wide-open eyes
I espied, a comely, crystal gurgling brook.

And marvelled at the natural wealth
Of his lavish family estate vast
And waited with inner trepidation
As his mother made her visitation.

And asked me how soon I could decide
To become her first born's suitable bride
I caressed the long stemmed rose he gave
The thorn upon my thumb did plant a stake.

I gazed upwards and blinding clear
Warned the words of Shakespeare,
"By the pricking of my thumb,
Something evil this way comes!"

And I lowered my eyes in soft regret
I acknowledged, how bitterly I'd come to hate
The gilded life of the caged bird
Her son's heart now young, would harden fast,
And like the elegant couch he sat me on
I would become,
Decorous furniture in a lifeless room.

I arose, my palms crushed his sweet velvet rose
I smiled, replied, "A bride? I want a career first,
Your son may wait for me, if so, he chose."

Her eyes crystallised, lips, a thin firm line,
"Young lady, you choose water over vintage wine.
A family name, an illustrious ancestral line,
What's in a career over a lineage fine?'

My eyes shone soft waters she so descried,
Water, the elixir of human lives,
Your wine of intoxicating pedigree
Will neither quench my thirst nor resurrect me."

The house so quiet, a stately tomb, opened
The sepulchre of its womb, into life's sunshine
I departed numb; my suitor walked me
To the gates, his eyes filled, with a pain
Too dumb.

I could not have saved a heart that loves its cage
Staying now, would defer betrayal to a later stage.
I remember his eyes still, how I rolled the dice
Of what mere destiny could never decide.
How in search of truth I discarded lies,
And left the rose of happily ever after prose
For the daring poem, of once upon a time.

AMRITA VALAN
Mercy

I caress, stroke the keyboard
My fingers try to feel the
Soul of each letter,
To describe mercy,
Is no mean feat.

For she sways
Still observes
Our crushed
Defeat
Half dead
Exhausted
Hopeless
As we grieve

She smiles
On our pain drilled
Tear filled eyes
Destiny's
Handmaiden
Fate's iron will.

But softer than
Air or
Water
Her elemental influence
Turns our h
Hopelessness
Into resolve
A state of grace.

She exudes her mercy
Most
When we kneel
Surrender
Accept our state.

Who weeps for us
It is she,
Who wipes our tears
With soft zephyr breeze
She who says
The fears are real
But you can and will

Deal with them,
Dear child
Of destiny.

PETROS KYRIAKOU VELOUDAS
'Moon Pocket'

'Inrainy You fill
in your watery eyes
float nostalgicunspeakable
moments of
impulses ...
I do not know if within
your psyche
storm
storm or your
refuge is born? ...
Fortunately, the umbrella
of my conscience
is always open
to rainy and snowy
emotions.
Listena sweet melody
of the song I
wrote for you, caressing
your ears a sea of
peace, serenity
mood
songs ..
Do not talk to the storm
prayer
is silent
Do you Think you do not hear the
sky?
The omniscient feelings as a
hears everything
and at the right time
provides solutions
do not waste
your heart
On palpitations
disposable emotional
ties
to the face now
that I read the happiness
Please do not
invite loneliness
and Cairns nectar
Bitter consumption of wine ..
Every time
To decreases

The full moon.
Look! the moon
crosses the back
of your mind a
pocket of ideas
Now before saying goodbye
I cause you a surprise
in your hair the kiss of hope
Look in the bag
I gave you
something that I forgot ..
Yes, I remembered
in your bag I
forgot about me. . smile!

JULENE TRIPP WEAVER
The Addition of Audience: A Meditation

this is my coming out poem
and you may think you know what that means
but I am coming out by adding you to a sacred circle
so please bow your head
let it drop slowly—
allow your neck to stretch
feel the small cracklings,
feel whatever else there is to feel

now that you feel yourself
stay inside for a minute
this is my invitation
this is my addition of you into my life,
feel how you react to what I have to tell you.

you might think you know what it is

slowly raise your head
still feeling your neck
let us look at each other

what I have to say is not easy
but I must get it out
it has been locked inside a long time
all I want from you is to witness
while staying fully with your own feelings
and please for the moments after
keep your reactions silent within you
let them bounce

this is a serious coming out poem
and I am gradually preparing you;
since you barely know me it may not matter
I don't want you to distance yourself from me
remember we perhaps have more in common than different
I live, eat, go to work, pay bills,
enjoy going out with friends—brace yourself

I am one of you
and I have AIDS.
let's sit together with you knowing this
sit fully with yourself
seeing me, as I could be you, living with AIDS
what does it feel like?

I feel vulnerable,
but I have come to feel it is necessary
to be honest
not that I haven't been honest
but I've had a veil on
For safety, and this
right now, does not feel safe

Where are you as I add you into my life?
When was your last HIV test?
Do you think you need one?
No? Well neither did I,
the time between the test and the result was easy
because I didn't believe I would be positive

then I got the news
what fell into place
is that this truly is a lifetime about death
about remembering the names of the dead
about my loss of soul and a death wish
since the day my father died;
it is a spiritual journey.

Knowledge does not make
us change our behavior
does not change our sexual fantasies

living with HIV/AIDS
I grieve the loss of full indulgence

I will always be a ball of contradictions
touching many points that don't exist.

Please slow down,
feel my news in your skin
how it affects you
I invite you to breathe
take time to feel the sensations
sit silent with me.

truth be bold—Serenading Life and Death in the Age of AIDS, *Finishing Line Press,* 2017

KARI WERGELAND
Waystation

COVID-19 challenge:
flip a fried egg perfectly
over easy.
One was close.
Most break and I eat the runny part
mixed with rumpled white.
It probably tastes the same,
especially when squished between halves
of an English muffin,
one with toasted cheese.
Sometimes I add little sausage links
and the meal becomes a flavor blast.
I never cooked over easy during the busy time,
rarely ordered it when I went out.
Now the clear jelly fish dying in a hot skillet,
turning white around its lone yellow eye
(before it's time to flip),
has become an obsession.
What do restaurants do
when the cook produces some folded creature
that could never sit pretty on a plate?
Do they fire her
when the number of grotesque eggs
becomes too high
(in relation to perfect flat white mounds
refusing to break till a fork hits)?
Are they forced to eat their failures
the way I do in the morning
sitting in the black Poang chair staring
at the green bushes blocking the tracks?
Though I can see the top of the train
whenever it rolls past.

JOHN YAMRUS
i remember the last time

my mother
combed my hair.

i was standing in
the kitchen with my friend Stephen

(it was always Stephen, never Steve)

and
we were
getting ready
to go back out to play.

i don't
remember how old i was,

i just remember
being sweaty and dirty

and i'd washed my face
and got a drink

and
i asked
my mother
to comb my hair
and i remember the way
Stephen looked at me when
she held the comb under the water

and ran it thru my hair.

i looked at the floor.
i heard the water running in the sink.

i felt
young and
stupid and ashamed.

the sink was
cold against my skin,

and there was
something cooking on the stove.

that was
also the last time
she knelt down and tied my shoes.

S.A. YITTA
Beyond Whitened Skin

To groom or be groomed - never a crime,
neither is a choice to cream just to glow,
but scraping skin in delight to fault frame.

Mirror's spoken evil of nature's game;
then races to peel the rare pearl follow,
coveting others' own image to fake form.

Endowed skin that won't sore in extreme;
yet, greed to be goddesses endlessly grow,
to please the world that outlives its norm.

Repulse for finer inner versions to maim
melanin that enriches the skin to glow.
Alas! mercury weaponry with prices come:

Self-esteem sacrificed to form in its prime,
dermis sores, eroding skin thickness so slow;
tender to cuts, bruises - thus infections brim.

Yet thousands clinch to the act to dare its grim:
comes wrinkles that wrap the skin - slow though;
and burns that many bear as skin starts to inflame.

What lies beyond whitened skin's beam?
Patches of colors as though suffering vitiligo?
What's more esthetic than nature's esteem!

EWA MARIA ZELENAY
A handbag

I am a lady's handbag...
    an unfashionable choice
    a shabby diary
    the only faithful friend
    assistance in likely events
    an infinite gallery of women's curiosities
    with a bunch of keys to magical locks
I am a lady's handbag...
    a redundant shopping list
    a carmine lipstick
    a dry cleaning bill
    a code that codes nothing
    a PIN which does not pin
    a non-identifying ID card
I am a lady's handbag...
    an envelope with an unwritten letter
    a sender who does not send
    an address with no addressee
I am a lady's handbag...
    an eternal quill pen from Adam's wing
    a disposable lighter without gas
    an eye that won't clip anything together anymore
I am a lady's handbag...
    ...found on the railroad tracks

BIOGRAPHIES

Sarfraz Ahmed
Sarfraz Ahmed lives and works in East Midlands, UK, and is a careers adviser, branching out as trainer, assessor, and a careers writer. He has been writing poetry for over eighteen years and has contributed to many anthologies, including Paint the Sky with Stars, published by Re-invention UK and many others published by the United Press, and many online contributions. His published books include poetry debut Eighty-Four Pins (June 2020) and My Teachers an Alien! (November 2020) which is a children's book with illustrator Natasha Adams. Green Cat Books. published both books https://green-cat.co/books He has published his second collection of poetry, along with Annette Tarpley, Two Hearts (February 2021). Sarfraz moderates the large Passion of Poetry group on Facebook and has a following on Facebook and Instagram. We can find him at open mic events, has shared his poetry globally, including the New York circuit.

Barth Akpah
Dr. Bartholomew C. Akpah (pen name, Barth Akpah), is an Associate Professor and Chair of the Department of Languages and Literature, William V. S Tubman University, Harper, Liberia. He is a literary critic; his critical essays have been published in reputable journals. His debut collection, *Land of Tales*, is on the reading list of some higher academic institutions in Nigeria and beyond.

Keith Allison
Keith Allison is a father and an educator. He is the author of two books, Screaming with My Indoor Voice (poetry and essays, 2020) and What if the Shoe Were on the Other Hoof? (essays and artwork, 2015). He uses poetry to express his hopes for a more just and compassionate world for humans and nonhumans alike. Poetry also allows him to vent his frustrations when we seem so far from accomplishing those goals. Keith also compiles and edits a video poetry collection, Outdoor Voices in an Indoor World, that brings together many amazing poetic voices and can be found on YouTube. You can follow Keith's work on his blog, Ruminations of an Angry Cow, at angrycowpoetry.blogspot.com or reach him at angrycowpoetry@gmail.com.

Pamela Anderson
Pam Anderson is a poet, lover of blues music, traveler, hiker, and yoga practitioner who grew up in Warren, Ohio, in an area once known as The Steel Valley. Much of her writing focuses on the Holocaust, reflecting stories her father recounted from his service as a paratrooper in the 82nd Airborne during WWII. Her Holocaust poem "My Brother's Coat" won the Association of Writers and Writing Program Intro Journals Project Award. Her chapbook Just the Girls: A Kaleidoscope of Butterflies; A Drift of Honeybees was published by The Poetry Box press. Widow Maker was published by Finishing Line Press. And her collection of poems for children-- The Galloping Garbage Truck—was published by Kelsay Books/Daffydown Dilly Press. She holds an MA in English Literature from Kent State University and an MFA from the Northeast Ohio Master of Fine Arts Program (NEOMFA), which awarded her a Bisbee (Arizona) Travel and Study Fellowship. She has been a ghostwriter, grants writer, and fundraiser for public radio. When she is not traveling with her husband to far-flung places to snap pictures of windows, doors, and lightbulbs, you can find her in Northeast Ohio and Charlotte, North Carolina. She has never watched Baywatch, nor does she own a red bathing suit.

Madeline Artenberg,
New York City-based writer, was a photojournalist and street theatre performer before falling for poetry. Her work has appeared in many publications, such as Rattle and The POET. She was semi-finalist in Margie, The American Journal of Poetry contest, and finalist in the Mudfish 2020 contest. One of her poems was nominated as Best of the Net 2020 by Poets Wear Prada. For many years, she has been co-producing The Alternative New Year's Day Poetry Extravaganza.

Jan Ball
Jan's 349 published poems have appeared in various journals, inclusing: ABZ , Mid - American Review and Parnassus . Three chapbooks and one full length poetry collection, I Wanted to Dance With My Father , were published by Finishing Line Press. Orbis, England, nominated her for the prestigious Pushcart Prize in 2020. Jan was a Franciscan nun from 1960 to 1967 then lived in Australia for fourteen years with her Aussie husband and two children. She completed a dissertation at The University of Rochester: Age and Natural Order in Second Language Acquisition (1996) then taught ESL at Rochester Institute of Technology, and, back in Chicago, Loyola and DePaul Universities. Now, when not gardening at their farm, Jan and her husband like to cook for their friends.

Les Bernstein
Author of Naked Little Creatures, Amid the Din, Borderland and And Yet, lives in Mill Valley, California with her family of 15. Les has recently taken her poems out of her pockets and desk drawers.

Bengt o Björklund
The poet, artist, journalist, photographer, writer, musician and editor Bengt O Björklund was born in Stockholm 1949. In 1968 he landed in jail in Istanbul for $ 20 worth of hash and met a bunch of international artists, poets and musicians. It was then he embarked on his artistic voyage in many directions as well as learning to cook, do yoga and generally get a life.

Lin Marshall Brummels
grew up at the edge of the Nebraska Sandhills. Brummels earned a Psychology BA from the University of Nebraska-Lincoln and a MS in Rehabilitation Counseling from Syracuse University. After retiring from a counseling career at Wayne State College, in Wayne, Nebraska Brummels started a private counseling practice where she works as a Nebraska licensed mental health counselor. She's published poems in journals, magazines, and anthologies. She served as a Poetry Out Loud judge at the Northeast Nebraska Regional Semi- Finals of Poetry Out Loud, for several years and online in 2020. Her poetry chapbooks are "Cottonwood Strong" and "Hard Times," a 2016 Nebraska Book Award winner. Her book of poems, "A Quilted Landscape," was published in 2021.

Troy Camplin
Troy Camplin is a poet, fiction writer, and playwright living with his wife and three children in Richardson, TX. He has a B.A. in recombinant gene technology from Western Kentucky University; a M.A in English from the University of Southern Mississippi, where he studied fiction under Frederick Barthelme; and a Ph.D. in the Humanities from the University of Texas at Dallas, where he studied fiction under Robert Nelsen and poetry under Frederick Turner. He is the author of the novella Hear the Screams of the Butterfly and Diaphysics, a work of philosophy. He has also had also had several poems, short stories, and scholarly papers and book chapters published. His play Almost Ithacad won first place at the HUB Theater's Cyberfest playwriting festival.

Taniya Chakraborty

Author of seven books of poetry was born on **Name: Taniya Chakraborty** November 22, 1990. **She lives at Rishra, a District- Hooghly in West-Bengal, India.**

Rick Christiansen

is a refugee from corporate America. After retiring a few years ago he returned to his first love of writing. His work can be found in the archives of Oddball Magazine online and on his Twitter Feed. His poem "George's Bloom" has been selected for the upcoming Spring 2021 edition of Muddy River Poetry Review. He will be a Featured Poet for the Uncloistered Poetry Zoom Event on 5-9-21. He lives in the heart of darkness to be found in the middle Middle West with his basset hound Annie. His father always said to be sure you leave a hole when you are gone. He is filling that hole with words.

Todd Cirillo

has been called "the best American poet writing clean, honest lines". He is co-founder and editor of Six Ft. Swells Press and one of the originators of the After-Hours Poetry movement. His latest book is, Kisses From A Straight Razor (Epic Rites Press, 2020). Other books include; Sucker's Paradise, Burning the Evidence, ROXY, Three For the Road, Everybody Knows the Dice Are Loaded, Still a Party, This Troubled Heart, Sexy Devils and more. Todd has performed across the United States and his poems have appeared in numerous national and international literary journals, magazines and cocktail napkins everywhere. Todd lives in New Orleans, Louisiana where he seeks out shiny moments and strange wisdom. He can be found at www.toddcirillo.com

Davide Rocco Colacrai

Davide Rocco Colacrai (born in Switzerland) is a Legal expert and an Italian poet. Since 2008 he has won more than thousand literature awards and has published nine books - the last one "From the same substance of our fathers" this year. He loves reading, playing piano and harp, collecting 7" singles (he has two thousand pieces from all around the world) and walking with his dog Mitty.

Pat Connors

Pat Connors first chapbook, Scarborough Songs, was published by Lyricalmyrical Press in 2013, and charted on the Toronto Poetry Map. Part Time Contemplative, his second chapbook with Lyricalmyrical, was released in 2016. He contributed 18 poems to Bottom of the Wine Jar, published by SandCrab books in 2017, and launched in Cuba. He was nominated for the 2011 Best of the Net contest, as well as the 2012 and 2013 Fermoy International Poetry competitions in Ireland. His poetry articles and book reviews have been published in Canada and Belgium, and read worldwide. He was literary juror for Big Art Book 2013 by Scarborough Arts. He was one of the organizers of the Great Canadian PoeTrain Tour in April, 2015. His poetry has appeared in Aquillrelle Magazine, Harbinger Asylum, Tyndale (College) Poetry Anthology, Ambassador XV, Poetry Pacific, Canadian Stories, Lummox anthologies 6-9, Northern Voices Journal, Big Pond Rumours, VerseAfire, The Friendly Voice, Lakeview International Journal, Juniper, Artis Magazine, Poetry'Z Own Magazine, Labour of Love, the anthology of the 25th Austin International Poetry Festival, Wax Poetry, Silver Birch Press, Umbrella, The 55 Project, among other publications and online entities. He is a manager for the Toronto chapter of 100,000 Poets for Change. His first full collection, The Other Life, has been released by Mosaic Press, and is available for pre-order on the Barnes & Noble website.

Lorraine Currelley
Lorraine Currelley, poet, writer, storyteller, mental health counselor, human rights and mental health advocate, is the founder & director of Poets Network & Exchange. A positive and supportive space for poets and writers of all levels, where she facilitates poetry and creative writing workshops and produces poetry readings, writing workshops and literary events. She is published in numerous poetry and literary anthologies and publications. Lorraine Currelley is the former first and only president of The Harlem Arts Fund. Currelley co-founded and organizes annual Bronx Book Fair in the Bronx, NY.

Kate Cumiskey
Kate Cumiskey is a writer, painter, and social justice activist in coastal Florida. Her work appears regularly in fine literary and peer-reviewed journals. Cumiskey and her husband Mikel work together to meet the needs of homeless teenagers and young adults by housing them and promoting public awareness, including founding an independent student cadre at a local high school. She is recognized by the state of Florida Department of Education as a Distinguished Educator through the Best and Brightest Scholarship program, and as a pioneering Autism advocate by the National Association of Social Workers. This is Cumiskey's fourth book.

Bill Cushing
Bill Cushing earned an MFA from Goddard College. His 2019 book A Former Life from Finishing Line Press was honored with a Kops-Featherling International Book Award. Bill 's chapbook Music Speaks won the San Gabriel Valley Poetry Festival, then medaled in the 2021 New York City Book Award. His latest chapbook of poems, . . .this just in. . ., was released in July 2021.

Mahua Das
is an excellent elocutionist, painter, poet and writer. She has presented herself as a host in many renowned tv channels(Sadhana Bangla, Doordarshan,24 ghonta, Mon sangeet, Tara Tv, CTVN ,Spandan Bangla and many other channels) of Kolkata (India). She is an excellent performer. She writes poems and articles in many magazines,little magazines,newspapers,web mag of India and Bangladesh. She worked as content writer in Relax Radio(London). Very recently, in Columbia ,her poetries are translated in Spanish language. Mahua writes poems in Bengali ,and translates those in English also. She translated many poetries (from English to Bengali) of Wilmer Zuleta ,who resides in Columbia. Recently, she appeared as a guest in many international literary discussion session in many Facebook and you tube online programs. In Columbia ,they took two interview sessions on her. In Bangladesh , she takes classes on performing arts. She appeared as a jury in many competitions and shows across West Bengal,India.

Mili Das
is a bilingual poet from Kolkata, India. She also writes stories and novels, drama, features, cinema script, and loves to recite her own poetry. She writes in different Bengali magazines, periodicals published from India, Bangladesh, Germany, Colombia, Romania , Poland, Nigeria, Virginia, Spain, America, and Turkey Her first poetry book 'APEKSHA KORCHHI BANDI KAFINE' was published in January 2019. Demand for her lovely poems from common people all over India urged her to publish her second poetry book 'RAJBHABANER SAMNE' and third English poetry book "YOU ARE STILL THERE" published from Romania, 2021. Her fourth English poetry book "NEVER BROKEN" was published from Florida, USA. She was invited as a poet to Raj bhaban, the Governor house of West Bengal. She is an eminent recipe writer of West Bengal. She attended various TV programs on national as well as local TV channels.

She is regular recipe writer in different Bengali food magazines. She is now invited as a judge for various cooking competitions.

Nandita De

Writer/freelance journalist/ Senior Editor CC/housewife. Formerly with Economic Times. **Cover stories and Feature Writer** with Statesman, Illustrated Weekly, Economic Times, Telegraph, Times of India, Femina, Filmfare, Germany Today, Voix Meets Mode, UK, FrontierWeekly, Setu, Chrysanthemum Chronicles, Raven Cage, Taifas, OPA, Litterateur, Cultural Reverence, Poetry Planet, New York Parrot etc. **Co Author** in 38 anthologies including 3 books from Innerchildpress, 3 from Silk Road, Compassion, Paradise on Earth II and The Literary Parrot; and 5 Coffee Table Books. **Editor**: Macabre Tales and Demigods are Alive.

Nancy Dafoe

Author and educator Nancy Avery Dafoe writes across genres and has won multiple awards for her work, including the William Faulkner/William Wisdom creative writing competition in poetry (2016). She won first place in the international short story competition from New Century Writers and first prize in prose poetry from the Soul-Making Literary competition, among other awards. Dafoe has eleven published books, with her twelfth book coming out in September 2022.

Zlatan Demirovic

Zlatan Demirovic is a serial entrepreneur, book writer, poet, hypnotherapist, best known for his rapid-learning of self-healing techniques, helping clients to produce seemingly self-developing results in minimum time. The founder of "PRODIGY LIFE ACADEMY and author of the "PRODIGY LIFE PROGRAM", which serves as a platform for spiritual and personal development. President of ASSOCIATION OF ARTISTS AND WRITERS OF THE WORLD-SAPS for Balkan region and USA. Admin advisor for "Poetry and Literature World Vision" His poetry has been translated to many world languages, such as: Italian, French, Spanish, German, Swedish, Greek, Turkish, Chinese, Hindu, Bengal, BCS (Bosnian, Croatian, Serbian), Albanian, Hausa- Nigerianan, Arabic, Aleut (Alaska), Pakistan, Bahasa-Insonesia, Kurdish, Persian, Azerbaijan, Tajik and others (on the way). Zlatan was born, June, 23. 1958 in Sarajevo, Bosnia and Hercegovina. His art-orientation started in very early age, as a songwriter, guitar player, later, novelist. After finding his final refuge in USA, he started writing in English, where he published his books: "Prodigy Life" Vol 1,2,3., " 4 Steps Teaching of Self-healing" and "Genius MINDSET Training", on KDP AMAZON, and the final version, paperback "Prodigy Life", under pan name Dr. Goldy Brown, with Balboa Press, subdivision of Hay House, 2020. His poetry is participating many renowned international anthologies at the time. He is a sheaf editor of "Prodigy Published" USA, publishing and promoting books, self-developing programs and anthologies of world multilingual poetry.

Linda Trott Dickman

has been writing poetry since her first sleep-away camp experience when she was ten years old. She is a recently retired school librarian. Linda is the author of *Robes: The Art of Being Covered, The Air That I Breathe* and *Road Trip*. Linda's poetry has been published on-line, in several anthologies, an international journal. She is the current coordinator of poetry for the Northport Arts Coalition (Northport, NY.) Linda has been teaching poetry to children for over 35 years and leads a poetry workshop for adults at Samantha's Li'l Bit O' Heaven coffee house in East Northport, NY.

Casey Dorman
is a former university professor and dean, a psychologist, a literary review editor, an essayist, and the author of thirteen novels, a collection of short stories and poems, and three non-fiction books, including a volume in the Johns Hopkins Series on Neuroscience and Psychiatry . He has published academic and research articles in psychology, medical, public health and philosophy journals. He is a member of the Society of Philosophers in America. Casey's novels borrow heavily from his clinical and research background and his interest in cognitive neuroscience and span genres from mystery and science fiction to literary works. His science fiction tries to reflect recent hard science and raise philosophical and social issues at the same time. His most recent novel, Ezekiel's Brain, is a scifi novel on the cutting edge of research in neuroscience and artificial intelligence and addresses issues of ethics and ecology. Casey lives in California near the ocean and enjoys gardening, hiking, reading and wine- tasting with his wife.

Sherri Dratfield
graduated from Goucher College and is a member of the Phi Beta Kappa Society. She received an M.F.A. in Acting from the University of Denver and holds a J.D., with election to Order of the Coif, from New York University School of Law. Sherri's third collection of poetry, Millie Collins, Your Barn is Gone , was just published (February 2021) by Cervena Barva Press. Sherri's two previous collections of poetry, The City (Finishing Line Press, 2013) and Water Vigils (Finishing Line Press, 2014) were both nominated for a Pushcart Prize. Her poems have appeared in various journals and anthologies and have been awarded recognition in the Margaret Reid Contest for Traditional Verse, Jewish Currents' Raines Poetry Competition and the Passager Poetry Contest. Sherri lives in the West Village of Manhattan with her husband, Simon. They visit their shore home in Ventnor City, New Jersey during all seasons.

Rose Drew,
an economic migrant to the UK, is a book publisher and editor (Stairwell Books), a physical anthropologist often writing about those twin 19th century plagues: workhouses and TB, and a performance poet. Rose and partner Alan have hosted long-running open mic night York Spoken Word (lately via Zoom) since January 2006.

Robin Wyatt Dunn
was born in Wyoming in 1979. The son of a geologist father and a potter mother, he has lived in six states, the U.K., and Canada. New Pop Lit called him "one of the most talented writers in America." He has been nominated for several awards, including the Rhysling, Elgin, Pushcart and Best of the Net. He was once a finalist for Poet Laureate of Los Angeles. Currently he lives in Tucson, Arizona.

Alex R. Encomienda
is an author and editor of literary fiction, genre fiction, absurdist fiction and poetry. Alex has had work published in notable magazines including Dark Gothic Resurrected, Boulder Weekly, The 5th Wall Press and Adelaide magazine. Alex is also the Editor-In-Chief of the online triannual literary journal "Labyrinthine Passages". Alex often expresses ideas of theology, philosophy, escapism, existentialism and love in his work.

Deirdre Fagan
is a widow, wife, mother of two, and associate professor and coordinator of creative writing in the English, Literature, and World Languages Department at Ferris State University. Fagan is the author of the forthcoming memoir, Find a Place for Me, Regal House Publishing (2022), a collection of short stories, The Grief Eater, Adelaide Books (2020), a chapbook of poetry, Have Love, Finishing Line Press (2019),

and a reference book, Critical Companion to Robert Frost, Facts on File (2007). She is a poetry Pushcart nominee and her poem "Outside In" was a Best of the Net finalist in 2018. Fagan is the poetry editor for Orange Blossom Review and has also written academic essays on poetry, memoir, and pedagogy. Meet her at deirdrefagan.com

Peg Fox
Margaret A. Fox is a new poet. Her first collection of poems, *Touched by Stars*, was published by Finishing Line Press *(2019)*. She has read her poems at Tongue & Groove Midwest and most recently on Parrot Literary Corner New York. While living in New Jersey, she performed in New Jersey Opera Festival and Street Theater of Princeton. She received the *Mayor of Cincinnati Humanitarian Award (2016)*, and holds a M.A. degree in Interdisciplinary Studies and Social Science from Antioch University, Yellow Springs, OH.

Damon Freed
Damon Freed an artist who cherishes balance, reason, and ambiguity; and he expresses it through a variety of working methods, from abstracted realities to nonobjective paintings of grids, he believes reality exists on the edge of perception. And while his Dad has been his best and greatest influence Agnes Martin and Brice Marden's work are among them. He received his B.F.A. from the School of Visual Arts in New York City where he graduated with honors. Freed taught at two places for 10 years at the college level. His first year was in '09. His M.F.A. is from Hunter College, City University of New York. Freed has studied with such luminaries as Jack Whitten, Marilyn Minter, David Chow, Juan Sanchez, Sanford Wurmfeld, Tobi Kahn, Lucio Pozzi, Tim Rollins, Alice Aycock, Susan Crile, Anton van Dalen, Suzanne Anker, Donald Kuspit, Katy Siegel among others. He has been exhibited in galleries in New York City, Saint Louis, Kansas City and Columbia, Missouri. In writing, my influences are my mom and dad, sister and brothers, and friends, mostly. His inspirations are my family and dearest friends, and the people he meets in every direction! Freed has not been formally trained in poetry but is an avid writer of works and spoken word. He has nine books of poetry published by himself. He has been published by The Writer's Place online and by The Rye Whiskey Review. You may find his collections of poetry in the Sedalia Public Library as well. Freed may be reached at damonfreed@gmail.com or by going to his website online.

Cindy Frenkel
Cindy Frenkel's *The Plague of the Tender-Hearted* was recently released from Finishing Line Press. Her poetry is forthcoming in the anthologies *Divining Dante* and *Poets Speaking to Poets: Echoes and Tributes* . Her remembrance, *"Galway Kinnell and the Blue Button-Down,"* was in *The Southampton Review*. She served as a Writer-in-Residence with InsideOut Literary Arts Project (iO), which brings working poets into Detroit public schools; her essay 'Sharing Voices, Acting Crazy" is in the anthology *To Light a Fire*. Her writing has appeared in numerous places from *Vanity Fair* to *The New York Observer*, where she was a columnist. She also served as the writer/editor for the Detroit Institute of Arts magazine (*DIA*). A Hambidge fellow, for the past 12 years, Cindy has taught college; her essay "15 lessons from 9 years of teaching" appeared in *Writers in Education*. She is involved in animal rescue as well as suicide awareness and prevention. To learn more, please visit www.cindyfrenkel.com.

Madhu Gangopadhyay
Madhu Gangopadhyay hails from India. She is presently residing in Bangalore. Her passion for writing began when she was in school. She loves to pen down her musings at random moments. She is fiercely passionate about poetry and short stories, and her penchant for mythology can be seen in her works. She conveniently explores all the genres of poetry writing and has written on a plethora of topics. She has a Masters degree in English Literature from Calcutta University and a Bachelors degree in Education. She

has been in the education industry for two decades now. She has also been a content developer and has designed academic course books for senior school students and colleges. She had also been associated with one of the leading Print media houses in India. A soft skills trainer, motivational speaker, and an avid social worker: she is also an exponent of Indian classical dance forms, her passion since childhood.It is only this January that she launched herself into this virtual world of fascinating writers and poets. She has also written some short stories that have been published in Literoma. Her poems have been published in THE SILK ROAD, Mediterranean Waves, published from Cairo, OPA, Open Door Magazine,Paradise On Earth, Volume II(The Third Eye, Butterfly Press), Insignia, Academy of The Heart And Mind, and in various other online journals including Spillwords. Her works revolve around every human emotion, life as a whole, nature, and the universe. Right now I am into technical writing, apart from doing my MA in Psychology.

Shaswata Gangopadhyay
One of the Prominent face of Contemporary Bengali Poetry, who started writing in Mid 90s. Born and brought up at Kolkata, Shaswata has profound interest in travelling, adventure and classical music. Shaswata writes in Bengali, the 4th largest language of the earth and as per UNESCO, it is the sweetest language. His poems have been published in all major journals of Bengali literature. He has been invited to read his poems in different virtual poetry festivals of Europe and Both North and Latin America, like World Poetry festival in Argentina and Cuba, International Poetry festival in Greece. He had also participated in Silk Road Poetry festival in China. His poems are regularly published in all six continents through translations in different languages. His book of Poems: Inhabitant of Pluto Planet (2001), Offspring of Monster (2009), Holes of Red Crabs (2015) and Rhododendron Cafe (2021). Recently His 'Selected Love Poems' have been published from Cairo, Egypt.

Davidson Garrett
is a native of Shreveport, Louisiana. He trained for the theater at The American Academy of Dramatic Arts and graduated from The City College of New York in 1988, with an M.S. in Education. A member of Screen Actor's Guild/AFTRA and Actors' Equity, he has worked in theater, film and television since 1973. His poetry, fiction and articles have been published in The New York Times, The Episcopal New Yorker, Xavier Review (New Orleans), Sensations Magazine, Third Wednesday, Marco Polo Arts Mag, Big City Lit, the website of The Beat Museum in San Francisco and in Podium, the online literary journal of the 92nd Street Y. Davidson is the author of the poetry collection: "King Lear of the Taxi" published by Advent Purple Press. Poetry from that collection was featured in the short film "Taxi Driver" by Flashgun Films of Great Britain, which was screened at London's Portabello Film Festival in 2008. In 2011, Davidson was nominated for a Pushcart Prize and in May 2013, he was invited to read at Joe's Pub in New York City as part of the Taxi Drivers' Workshop for the PEN World Voices Festival. His chapbook, "To Tell The Truth I Wanted To Be Kitty Carlisle and Other Poems" was published in 2013 by Finishing Line Press. In 2014, Davidson was awarded 1st Prize from the 2nd Annual Juanita Torrence-Thompson International Poetry Award sponsored by Amulet Poetry Magazine. In 2015, Advent Purple Press published his latest chapbook, "Southern Low Protestant Departure: A Funeral Poem." In 2016, excerpts from the funeral poems were published in the literary journal, 2 Bridges Review, from the City University of New York. In 2017, Advent Purple Press published Davidson's newest chapbook, "What Happened to The Man Who Taught Me Beowulf and Other Poems." In 2020, Kelsay Books published his collection of poems, "Arias of a Rhapsodic Spirit." All of his books are available on amazon. Davidson is a retired New York City taxi driver who drove for 40 years to help subsidize his art.

Kathie Giorgio

is the author of five novels, two story collections, an essay collection, and two poetry chapbooks. A full-length poetry collection, No Matter Which Way You Look, There Is More To See, was just released in September 2020. Her new novel, All Told, will be released in late 2021 by Austin Macauley Publishers. A poetry chapbook, Olivia In Five, Seven, Five; Autism In Haiku, will be released in early 2022 by Finishing Line Press. She's been nominated for the Pushcart Prize in fiction and poetry and awarded the Outstanding Achievement Award from the Wisconsin Library Association, the Silver Pen Award for Literary Excellence, the Pencraft Award for Literary Excellence, and the Eric Hoffer Award In Fiction. She is the director and founder of the international creative writing studio, AllWriters' Workplace & Workshop LLC.

Robert Gibbons

Robert Gibbons is a 2016 Norman Mailer Fellow. He has published in Promethean, Suisun Valley Review, Inner Child Press, Program, Brooklyn Poets, Turtle Island Quarterly, Deep Literary, and many online anthologies. His first collection of poetry, Close to the Three, was published by Three Rooms Press in 2012. Roberts also contributed to international anthologies on peace and gender violence. Among these anthologies are: Intercontinental Anthology of Poetry on Universal Peace (2014), Mandela Tributes (2014) - both edited by Yayati Madan G Gandhi and Mutiu Olawuyi, to mention a few.

Ted Guevara

Ted Bernal Guevara has a new collection of poetry, entitled Nice . Mr. Guevara resides in South Carolina, where he is a freelance writer. He is the author of two James Dean conceptual novels, Days of Slint and Lips of a Mastodon . His first novel, A Circle with Two Corners , won praises from Midwest reviews, including one from The Sentinel. The crime-romance novel, True Feel, is in its Second Edition. Ted has also published three other volumes of poetry, Films , Birds on Elephant , and Tonto and Destinata. Although he delves into an array of themes, always looking for the unusual and the edgy, Guevara finds adherence in the plight of the disabled and all their "profound richness," as he states in a poem. At age 9, his family moved from the Philippines to Marion, Indiana— where all his physical challenges were realized and at the same time, rewarded. His physician father never taught him how to dribble a basketball but had trained him to type a thousand words per day--from notable books--to increase his typing speed. Ted caught the literary bug instead, from the exercise. Kirkus considers Mr. Guevara as Author to Watch in 2018. Asphalt & Water , the third JD novel, will be out in late 2022.

John Guzlowski

John Guzlowski's writing appears in Garrison Keillor's Writer's Almanac, North American Review, Rattle, Ontario Review, Salon.Com, and many other journals. His poems and personal essays about his Polish parents' experiences as slave laborers in Nazi Germany and refugees making a life for themselves in Chicago appear in his award-winning memoir Echoes of Tattered Tongues (Aquila Polonica Press). He is also a columnist for the Dziennik Zwiazkowy (the oldest Polish language daily in America) and the author of Suitcase Charlie and Little Altar Boy, noir mystery novels set in Chicago.

Faleeha Hassan

She is a poet, teacher, editor, writer, playwriter born in Najaf, Iraq, , who now lives in the United States. Faleeha is the first woman to wrote poetry for children in Iraq. She received her master's degree in Arabic literature, and has now published 25 books. Her poems have been translated into English, Turkmen, Bosevih, Indian, French, Italian, German, Kurdish, Spain, Korean, Greek, Serbia ,Albanian , Pakistani , Malayalam, and ODIA language. Ms. Hassan has received many awards in Iraq and throughout the

Middle East for her poetry and short stories. Faleeha Hassan has also had her poems and short stories published in a variety of American magazines .Faleeha Hassan. Pulitzer Prize Nomination 2018, PushCart Prize 2019 , IWA. She's the winner of the Moonstone Chapbook Contest 2019. The Iraq-USA Cultural Ambassador also won the Women of Excellence Inspiration award from SJ magazine 2020. Contact her at: d.fh88@yahoo.com

Damian Ward Hey
Damian Ward Hey's poetry has appeared in many journals, most recently The RavensPerch; e·ratio; Neologism; Jerry Jazz Musician; and Rat's Ass Review. He has also published with Heroin Love Songs; Cajun Mutt Press; Voices from the Fire; Black Flowers; Madness Muse Press; Formidable Woman Sanctuary; The Rye Whiskey Review; They're Conspiring against the Alien Buddha; and Birth - Lifespan Vol. 1. (Pure Slush). More will be published, shortly, in the anthologies, Poets with Masks On (Melanie Simms, Ed.); and milagros: easing the edges (d. ellis phelps, Ed.). Hey has a BA in English from Columbia University and a Ph.D. in Comparative Literature from Stony Brook University. For the past 25 years, he has been a professor of English on Long Island and is the founding editor of Stone Poetry Journal. stonepoetryjournal.com.

Layeba Humanity,
a natural bilingual English/Hindi Poetess/Motivator, from North India. She is M.Sc. in Zoology with great command over human psychology. She is an honourable member of World Nations Writers Union and featured with some magazines. She writes truth and raises social issues in her writings as well as she has worked as guest poet in radio stations. She has been a fighter of adverse situations and narrow mind-set She is making a mark among all over world literature and only believes in humanism with a sound of justice and truth. She is active on social platforms and started YouTube channel of Literature/Motivation- https://youtube.com/c/LayebasworldAuthor She wishes more acceleration in the wings of literature through exact view.

Dionne Hunter
Dionne D Hunter is originally from Birmingham, Alabama, but has also called Ohio and North Carolina home. After the sudden death of her mother, Ms. Hunter was raised by her widowed father, who strove to raise her to be self-reliant and proud of her African American heritage. He also encouraged her to read; and read she did, everything including poetry, sci fi, horror and romance. She fell in love with the art of storytelling and would spend hours weaving adventurous tales to entertain her siblings. As a United States Navy Veteran, mother of 2 and grandmother of 4, Ms. Hunter has gravitated to Spoken Word as an expression of her emotions and ideals. Her work has been included in anthologies published by Writing Knights, The Poet's Haven, and Crisis Chronicles Press. She has been featured in a web-series, Equity in Art: Cleveland Poet Speaks to Social Injustice as well as being featured during a television segment called How Art Speaks in Unsettling Times – Carolina Impact PBS Charlotte WTVI In addition, her Spoken Word videos have been selected to be screened during the 9th International Video Poetry Festival in Athens, Greece, and the 2021 Raleigh Films and Art Festival in North Carolina. Most recently she has authored a book titled "I am a Dahomey Warrior!" It follows the gripping journey of a young girl coming of age prior to the colonization of Africa and is written as a short story using poetry as an aid to enhancing the reader's journey.

Rachael Ikins

published three books with Finishing Line Press, "Transplanted", "God Considered the Horizon" and "Historias: stories of survival." She also did an honorarium workshop in Lismore, Ireland. Since then she has published two other poetry books and a mixed genre memoir with Clare Songbirds Publishing.

Larry Jaffe

Larry Jaffe is an internationally known and an award-winning writer, author and poet. For his entire professional career, Jaffe has been using his art to promote human rights. He was the poet-in-residence at the Autry Museum of Western Heritage, a featured poet in Chrysler's Spirit in the Words poetry program, co-founder of Poets for Peace (now Poets without Borders) and helped spearhead the United Nations Dialogue among Civilizations through Poetry project which incorporated hundreds of readings in hundreds of cities globally using the aesthetic power of poetry to bring understanding to the world. Jaffe impacts audiences and readers with a rich emotional range, masterfully crafted, written from the heart and soul with clarity and understanding. His work has been translated into over a dozen different languages. Jaffe has read his work in such distinguished locations as the Japanese American Museum, the Hammer Museum, the Museum of Tolerance, the Jewish Museum and the Museum of Literature in Prague and the Dylan Thomas Centre in Wales. He was the recipient of the Saint Hill Art Festival's Lifetime of Creativity Award, the first time given to a poet and was past Poet Laureate for Youth for Human Rights, and Florida Beat Poet Laureate. He has five books of poetry: Unprotected Poetry, Anguish of the Blacksmith's Forge, One Child Sold, In Plain View, 30 Aught 4, Sirens and the soon to be published Man without Borders . Jaffe's recent human rights activities include workshops and seminars on artist rights, human rights and human trafficking. He spends much of his time with his wife Shelley at their Scone Age Bakery & Café and has recently inaugurated a monthly poetry series – The Great Coffee House Poetry Reading Revival. Along with James Paul Wagner he is the editor for the Florida Bards poetry book series.

Pavol Janik

Mgr. art. Pavol Janik, PhD., (magister artis et philosophiae doctor) was born in 1956 in Bratislava, where he also studied film and television dramaturgy and scriptwriting at the Drama Faculty of the Academy of Performing Arts (VSMU). He has worked at the Ministry of Culture (1983–1987), in the media and in advertising. President of the Slovak Writers' Society (2003–2007), Secretary-General of the SWS (1998–2003, 2007–2013), Editor-in-Chief of the literary weekly of the SWS Literarny tyzdennik (2010–2013). Honorary Member of the Union of Czech Writers (from 2000), Member of the Editorial Board of the weekly of the UCW Obrys-Kmen (2004–2014), Member of the Editorial Board of the weekly of the UCW Literatura – Umeni – Kultura (from 2014). Member of the Writers Club International (from 2004). Member of the Poetas del Mundo (from 2015). Member of the World Poets Society (from 2016). Director of the Writers Capital International Foundation for Slovakia and the Czech Republic (2016–2017). Chief Representative of the World Nation Writers' Union in Slovakia (from 2016). Ambassador of the Worldwide Peace Organization (Organizacion Para la Paz Mundial) in Slovakia (from 2018). Member of the Board of the International Writers Association (IWA BOGDANI) (from 2019). He has received a number of awards for his literary and advertising work both in his own country and abroad. This virtuoso of Slovak literature, Pavol Janik, is a poet, dramatist, prose writer, translator, publicist and copywriter. His literary activities focus mainly on poetry. Even his first book of poems *Unconfirmed Reports* (1981) attracted the attention of the leading authorities in Slovak literary circles. He presented himself as a plain-spoken poet with a spontaneous manner of poetic expression and an inclination for irony directed not only at others, but also at himself. This style has become typical of all his work, which in spite of its critical character has also acquired a humorous, even bizarre dimension. His manner of expression is becoming terse to the point of being aphoristic. It is thus perfectly natural that Pavol Janik's literary interests should come to embrace aphorisms founded on a shift of meaning in the form of puns. In his work he is gradually raising some very disturbing questions and pointing to serious problems concerning the further development of humankind, while all the time widening his range of themes and styles. Literary experts liken Janik's poetic virtuosity to that in the work of Miroslav Valek, while in the opinion of the Russian poet, translator and literary critic, Natalia Shvedova, Valek is more profound and Janik more inventive. According to Sarita Jenamani, Secretary-General of the PEN International's Austrian Centre, Pavol Janik has his place in world literature. He has translated in poetic form several collections of poetry and written works of drama with elements of the style of the Theatre of the Absurd. Pavol Janik's literary works have been published not only in Slovakia, but also in Albania, Argentina, Austria, Bangladesh, Belarus, Belgium, Bosnia and Herzegovina, Bulgaria, Canada, Chile, Croatia, the Czech Republic, France, Germany, Hungary, India, Israel, Italy, Jordan, Kazakhstan, Kosovo, Kyrgyzstan, Macedonia, Mexico, Moldova, Nepal, Pakistan, Poland, the People's Republic of China, the Republic of China (Taiwan), Romania, the Russian Federation, Serbia, Singapore, South Korea, Spain, Syria, Turkey, Ukraine, United Kingdom, the United States of America, Uzbekistan, Venezuela and Vietnam.

Jake St. John

lives in the woods on the edge of the Salmon River. He is the author of several collections of poetry including Night Full of Diamonds (Whiskey City Press, 2021), Snow Moon (Holy & Intoxicated Publications, 2019) and Lost City Highway (A Jabber Publication, 2019). He is the former co-editor of Flying Fish and the former editor of Elephant. He is considered an original member of the New London School of poetry. His poems have appeared in print and online journals around the world.

Zaneta Vernado Johns

Zaneta Varnado Johns is the author of **Poetic Forecast**: *Reflections on Life's Promises, Storms, and Triumphs. She* co-authored **Voices of the 21st Century**: Resilient Women Who Rise and Make a Difference and **Jane Austen's** *an anthology of thoughts & opinions*
For more information about her, visit **www.zanexpressions.com**

pj johnson Poet Laureate of the Yukon

On Canada Day July 1st 1994, pj Johnson, the daughter of a Yukon trapper, was formally invested and given the title Poet Laureate of the Yukon during a ceremony in Whitehorse and became the first officially-invested poet laureate in Canada. As an oral/visual artist from a northern storytelling culture her poems, stories, plays and songs have been televised and performed at various venues across Canada and around the world. Her creative works have been published in books and journals globally; translated into several languages, and published widely. Diagnosed with a learning disorder called 'Nonverbal Learning Disorder' or NLD in 2005, pj johnson encourages people with a learning disability to realize they can still pursue their dreams. Active in the arts for decades as an oral/visual storyteller, mentor and performer at various venues across Canada, johnson is also an author, playwright, actor, musician, composer, teller of stories and Yukon ambassador. – If it's creative she's probably been there. Known as the Yukon Raven Lady, in 1985 johnson led a successful campaign to have the northern raven declared the official symbol of the Yukon Territory. She is a passionate animal rights advocate currently campaigning to protect the northern sled dogs. On Canada Day July 1st 2021 pj johnson will celebrate her 27th anniversary as Poet Laureate of the Yukon. She is the longest-serving Poet Laureate in Canada. Her book "it's howlin' time!" about the life and times of a northern Canadian poet laureate is available at Mac's Fireweed Books and on Amazon. Her Official Website is at: https://www.yukonpoetlaureate.com/

Jill Sharon Kimmelman
is a Pushcart Prize nominee in poetry. She has been nominated for Best Of The Net 2018. Her publication credits include, Vita Brevis Press, Spillwords Press, Fine Lines, Love of Food magazine, Poetic Musings Ezine, Yasou! A Celebration Of Life Ezine, The Poet Magazine, ILA, The New York Parrot , Passion of Poetry , multiple anthologies since 2018, several back cover blurbs, & a delightful dozen, Sparrow Productions, poetry videos based on her poems. Let Peace In & The Stars I'm Wishing On , have been the basis for two original songs. Let Peace In was the framework for an extraordinary poetry video. A portion of the proceeds, from the sales of the iBook & the coffee-table poetry art book versions is guaranteed to an organization, in the USA, which rescues & trains dogs to become PTSD service dogs, a cause very dear to the poet's heart. Jill's passions include reading aloud, "cooking from the heart," theatre, lively book discussions, & photography of food & flowers. Her culinary arts background is evident throughout her poetry & in conversations. She lives in Delaware, USA with her husband Tim, & is a proud mother of her son Jordan.

Susan Ksiezopolski,
an award-winning writer has published two poetry books, "My Words" and "Writing for Change" as well as two writing aides "The Writer's Workbook" and recently launched "Fuel Your Creativity" illustrated by award winning artist Angela Chao. She was featured in Canadian Immigrant Magazine along with her poem "Canadian By Choice". Her work has also been published in various anthologies, magazines and on-line platforms. Susan is a graduate of the Humber School for Writers. She volunteered as a Lead Training Facilitator with the Writers Collective of Canada (WCC) an organization that encourages voice and illuminates undiscovered strength in vulnerable communities. In 2019 and 2020, Susan lead the WCC's "Write Around Mississauga" initiative to expand programming within Mississauga through the Hazel McCallion Foundation for Arts, Culture and Heritage and Community Foundation of Mississauga. She developed *The Writer's Workshop, Write to Heal, Creative Resilience* and *Write Your Story*, and delivers these transformational workshops across the Greater Toronto Area. In 2018, Susan founded *WriteWell*, supporting organizations and individuals to unleash the creative power of writing and support their journey to wellness. In 2019 Susan was awarded the Mississauga Arts Council Fusion Grant in partnership with Angela Chao, to create Feel It! Exhibit a travelling interactive art show featuring seven unique art pieces integrating, music, art and poetry that expressed 7 core emotions. In 2020, with sponsorship from Mississauga Arts Council, Bell Canada, and the Ontario Trillium Foundation, Susan produced a short documentary "Art of Wellness – Creative Path to Mental Health", spotlighting the value of arts based programs for mental health and wellness. She is currently working on developing an eight week "Creative Resilience, Artful Way to Bounce" program incorporating poetry, art, music, dance and photography launching in September 2021. Visit Susan's website www.mywordsnow.com to find out more.

Janet Kozachek
is an internationally trained and exhibited artist. She received her Master of Fine Arts Degree from Parsons School of Design in New York, where she studied drawing and painting with Larry Rivers, Paul Resika, John Heliker, Leland Bell and poetry with J.D. McClatchy. Ms. Kozachek also lived, worked and studied in China for five years, including two years of graduate study at the the Central Academy of Fine Art in Beijing (CAFA), where she learned Chinese Poetry, Writing, Painting and Seal Carving. Ms. Kozachek has lived at various times in Europe, where she taught, painted and studied ceramics. In addition to her painting, Janet Kozachek is a well-known mosaic artist, and was the Founding President of the Society of American Mosaic Artists. Her work is in the collections of the Morris Museum of Art, The South Carolina State Museum, The Columbia Museum of Art, The I.P. Stanback Museum, The Calhoun County Museum and in numerous private collections. In 2020, Janet Kozachek received the Common Ground

on the Hill Award for Excellence in the Traditional Arts. She has received a category award in drawing from Art Fields 2018, a Puffin Foundation Award, National Endowment for the Arts subgrant awards, a Heritage Foundation Award, a Humanities Council Award and a Helena Rubinstein Scholar Award. She has published several articles, essays, poetry, and a book of illustrated rhymes for the cat, The Book of Marvelous Cats, and an illustrated poetry chapbook, My Women, My Monsters. Her full length illustrated poetry book, A Rendering of Soliloquies, Poetry for Figures Painted in Spots of Time, will be published by Finishing Line Press in 2022. Ms. Kozachek's art work has been featured at the Gibbes Museum of Art in Charleston, the South Carolina State Museum in Columbia, the I. P. Stanback Museum in Orangeburg, Richland County Library in Columbia, the Dupont Gallery in Virginia, the Stage Gallery in New York, the Mesa Center for Contemporary Art in Arizona, Eleven/Eleven Sculpture Gallery in Washington DC, and numerous others.

W. Ruth Kozak
is a Canadian travel journalist and writer with a strong interest in history and archaeology. A frequent traveller, Ruth lived for several years in Greece and instructs classes in travel journalist and creative writing. A travel writer since 1982, she is a regular contributor to EuropeUpClose www.europupclose.com . Until 2020, she published her own on-line travel zine at www.travelthruhistory.com . Her publications include articles in APA Insight Guides 1994, Writer's Abroad anthology "Foreign Flavours" as well as in three poetry anthologies and she was a writer for The Vancouver Guide for Planet Eye Traveler. Her ATHENS AND BEYOND e-book for Hunter Publishing, US was published in Nov 2015 on Kindle. She is the past president of the BC Association of Travel Writers. Ruth's first historical fiction novel SHADOW OF THE LION: BLOOD ON THE MOON (Volume One) was published July 2014 by www.mediaaria-cdm.com UK. Volume Two, BLOOD ON THE MOON: THE FIELDS OF HADES was published in January 2017. These are her first published literary works. Research was done in Greece and with the help of the Vancouver Greek Consul, the Ministry of Culture, Greece and the Society of Macedonian Studies, Thessaloniki, as well as help from various Classical scholars, and the Finnish Institute and Norwegian Institutes of Athens. A full version of SHADOW OF THE LION is available on Amazon Kindle. Her book of poetry ' SONGS FOR ERATO" poems written in Greece is published on Amazon.com. And Kindle. She is currently working on another historical novel, DRAGONS IN THE SKY a story that connects the Celts and the Greeks set in the 3rd Century BC.

R. Nikolas Macioci
earned a PhD from The Ohio State University, and for thirty years taught for the Columbus City Schools. In addition to English, he taught Drama and developed a Writers Seminar for select students. OCTELA, the Ohio Council of Teachers of English, named Nik Macioci the best secondary English teacher in the state of Ohio. Nik is the author of two chapbooks: Cafes of Childhood and Greatest Hits, as well as nine books: Why Dance, Necessary Windows, Cafes of Childhood (the original chapbook with additional poems), Mother Goosed, Occasional Heaven, A Human Saloon, Rustle Rustle Thump Thump, Rough, and Dark Guitar. Critics and judges called Cafes of Childhood a "beautifully harrowing account of child abuse," but not "sentimental" or "self-pitying," an "amazing book," and "a single unified whole." Cafes of Childhood was submitted for the Pulitzer Prize in 1992. In 2021, he was nominated for a Pushcart Prize and a Best of the Net Award. Forthcoming books are Stoney Seasons and A Feast of Losses. He is currently at work on My Hands Fell Empty. In addition, more than two hundred of his poems have been published here and abroad in magazines and journals, including Chiron, Concho River Review, The Bombay Review, Painted Bride Quarterly, The Comstock Review, and Blue Unicorn. He has won many awards including First Place in the 1987 National Writer's Union Poetry Competition, judged by Denise Levertov, First Place in The Baudelaire Award Competition, sponsored by The World Order of Narrative

and Formalist Poets (1989), Second Place in Zone 3's first annual Rainmaker Awards, judged by Howard Nemerov (1989), and Second Place in the Writer's Digest annual competition, judged by Diane Wakoski (1991).

Angie Mack
has lived and breathed creativity her entire life and has been employed as a leader in the arts for over 20 years. She is the author of Chronic Creativity: A Diagnostic Look at the Condition and How to Become Infected. Her heightened sense of creativity has led her to produce and direct over 100 musicals, two original poetry books and two original albums of music just to name a few. Most of her time is spent mentoring other musicians, leading teams for creative projects and advocating for dead blues musicians. Her international claim to fame is finding the unmarked grave of the Father of Ragtime Guitar, Arthur "Blind" Blake. She appears in many publications around the world for her advocacy and historical work surrounding Paramount Records which was based out of her hometown of Grafton, WI. Visit her online portfolio at https://angiemackreilly.com

Mike Matthews
is the author of a book titled, Water of Joy, published by Finishing Line Press. He has copies he can sign and then sell through PayPal, as well. His second book, Ashes , has been accepted to be published by Finishing Line Press. Ashes will be released in March, 2022, and it will be available on the publisher's page for ordering. Mike Matthews has been teaching college writing courses since 2001at Central Texas College in Killeen, Texas, including creative writing courses for writing poetry, short stories, and novels. He has sponsored the Writer's Club for students, and the student journal, Byways, for arts and letters, since soon after he arrived to teach at the community college. He has published several individual poems, including one titled "The City of Strings," in an anthology, The Book of Hopes and Dreams, (2006 edition) published in Scotland and still available on Amazon. He lives in a small city, Copperas Cove, in Texas. After classes, Mike Matthews goes for walks to the pond in the park to practice listening for the whispers that manifest the moments of poetry.

Joan McNerney
Joan McNerney's poetry is found in many literary magazines such as Seven Circle Press, Dinner with the Muse, Poet Warriors, Blueline, and Halcyon Days. Four Bright Hills Press Anthologies, several Poppy Road Journals, and numerous Poets' Espresso Reviews have accepted her work. She has four Best of the Net nominations. Her latest titles are *The Muse in Miniature* and *Love Poems for Michael* both available on Amazon.com and Cyberwit.net

Karla Linn Merrifield,
a nine-time Pushcart-Prize nominee and National Park Artist-in-Residence, has had 900+ poems appear in dozens of journals and anthologies. She has 14 books to her credit. Following her 2018 Psyche's Scroll (Poetry Box Select) is the 2019 full-length book Athabaskan Fractal: Poems of the Far North from Cirque Press. She is currently at work on a poetry collection, My Body the Guitar, inspired by famous guitarists and their guitars; the book is slated to be published in December 2021 by Before Your Quiet Eyes Publications Holograph Series (Rochester, NY). Her Godwit: Poems of Canada (FootHills Publishing) received the Eiseman Award for Poetry. She is a frequent contributor to The Songs of Eretz Poetry Review, and assistant editor and poetry book reviewer emerita for The Centrifugal Eye. She is a member of Just Poets (Rochester, NY), the Florida State Poetry Society, the New Mexico Poetry Society, and The Author's Guild. Visit her former blog, Vagabond Poet Redux, at http://karlalinn.blogspot.com. Tweet @LinnMerrifiel: https://twitter.com/LinnMerrifiel. Merrifield's photography has appeared in Outdoor,

Sea Stories, The Centrifugal Eye, among many magazines and publications. In fall 2000 High Falls Gallery in Rochester, NY, featured her bird photography in a one-woman show, Dawn of Migration and Other Audubon Dreams, and the Everglades National Park Coe Visitor Center presented a dozen of her photographs in its December 2011 exhibition of works by the park's artists-in-residence. She illustrated William Heyen's limited-edition 2012 The Green Bookcase with 50+ photographs. A second edition of the book was published in September 2018.

Frank Mottl
lives with his wife on the beautiful west coast of Canada. 'Mother's Keep' is his second book. Like his first book, 'The Cumberland Tales', it's a combo of prose and poetry with a poem preceding each chapter. Unlike 'The Cumberland Tales', 'Mother's Keep' has a linear plot and is based in the small town of Gibsons on the west coast of Canada during the depression years. When not writing, Frank enjoys sailing, maintaining his sailboat, and teaching English part time. Since retiring from the mill, Frank acquired his Bachelor of Arts - English Major from Thompson Rivers University and has spent a year in China teaching which was good fodder for his book, 'The Cumberland Tales.' Frank's wife, Linda, (who is an artist in her own right), painted the covers for both books, 'The Cumberland Tales' and 'Mother's Keep'. Frank is always ready to discuss literature having been a guest on various podcasts promoting his work. You can reach Frank through his website: www.frankwayne.net. There are two quotes which inspire Frank: The first by William Blake, and to paraphrase: 'My job is not to reason and compare, my job is to create'. The second quote is from John Keats, again to paraphrase: 'That which is creative must itself create.'

Mark A. Murphy
is an Ace poet, living with GAD, and OCD. He has poems forthcoming in Cultural Weekly and Acumen. He is a Pushcart Nominee, and has published seven books of poetry to date, including, 'Tin Cat Alley & Other Poems: Not to be Reproduced' by Venetian Spider Press, 2021. I have always thought that poetry can change lives, and still do. I believe artists have a responsibility to step up to the mark , and say the things, others, perhaps less privileged, would like to, or are unable to say. If humanity is to survive the current and impending ecological disaster beyond the next generation, we must learn new ways to live together, in harmony with nature., or we shall surely die together.

Elaine Nadal
A Pushcart Prize and Best of the Net-nominee, Elaine Nadal is the author of two poetry chapbooks: When and Sweat, Dance, Sing, Cut, published by Finishing Line Press. Her work has appeared in several journals, including Beyond Words Literary Magazine, Haunted Waters Press, Hoot Review, Grasslimb, and Latino Book Review Magazine.

Andrew Najberg
is author of The Goats Have Taken Over the Barracks (Finishing Line Press 2021). He is also the author of Easy to Lose (Finishing Line Press 2008). His poems have appeared in North American Review, Louisville Review, Mockingheart Review, Istanbul Review, Faultline Journal, Bangalore Review, Another Chicago Magazine, and many other journals and anthologies. His short fiction is forthcoming in Fleas on the Dog. Currently, he teaches creative writing for the University of Tennessee Chattanooga where he assists with the Meacham Writers Workshop. He graduated with an MFA from Spalding University.

Aji Ndumbeh Jobe
is a graduate of The Gambia College School of Education, a member of Victory Foundation and current mentee at Coaches of Influence Foundation. Her passion for writing and poetry gave her the opportunity

to become one of the finalists for The "Gambia's got talent 2019" event and Finalist of The Rising Star 2021. Additionally, her passion and skill in painting, led her to Win The UN75 Painting Competition on the theme: The Gambia we want in 2045 She emerged first (1st) position. Her passion for photography and poetry led to her recent accomplishments as 3rd place winner of the Oscar of African Creativity (ASWAN) award in Egypt, a graduate of The Tafla Leadership Academy, Finalist of The Rising Stars Africa under Poetry session participant of photography night in Senegal & Bamako, art exhibition in Khartoum Sudan and winner of Emerging Poet (YWAG). Her hobbies include painting, writing, speaking and photography and she desires to turn her photography hobby into a business.

Xrisa Nicolaki
Chryssa Nikolakis was born in Athens. She graduated from the University of Athens, Theology Department, with a Master's of the Arts; she has published literary studies in many scientific-theological journals. In 2017 she published her first poetry collection Sea Gate (Ostria). Her latest poetry book is Miracles and Fairies.

Chad Norman
lives beside the high-tides of the Bay of Fundy, Truro, Nova Scotia. He has given talks and readings in Denmark, Sweden, Wales, Ireland, Scotland, America, and across Canada. His poems appear in publications around the world and have been translated into Danish, Albanian, Romanian, Turkish, Italian, Spanish, Chinese, Czech, and Polish. His collections are Selected & New Poems (Mosaic Press), and Squall: Poems In The Voice Of Mary Shelley (Guernica Editions). And Simona: A Celebration of the S.P.C.A. came out early 2021 from Cyberwit.Net (India).

Isilda Nunes
was born in Portugal. She is a teacher, artist and an award-winning writer. Recently, she won the Intercontinental World Poetry Prize "Kairat Dusseinov Parman", the World Prize "Cesar Vallejo 2020" for Literary Excellence, the "Grito de Mujer Lisbon 2021 Award" and the World Prize "Aguila de Oro 2021" for Literary and Artistic Excellence. She has poems translated into Spanish, English, Hindi, Serbian, Polish and Mandarin and edited in Anthologies and Magazines in India, Bangladesh, Poland, Serbia, Brazil, Peru, Croatia, Greece, Republic of Seychelles and China. She is co-author of about forty national and international anthologies and solo books of poetry and prose, such as novels, short stories and manuals. She took part in Radio and Television programmes, book fairs and literary festivals. She is: The Collegiate World Executive President of the Union Hispanomundial de Escritores (UHE); World Ambassador of the Union Hispanomundial de Escritores (UHE); World Administrator of the Official Pages of the Union Hispanomundial de Escritores (UHE); Founding National President of the Union Hispanomundial de Escritores (UHE) in Portugal; Member of the WNWU (World Nation Writer's Union); Member of the "World Festival of Poetry" (WFP) and part of the Organizing Committee of this Festival in Portugal; Honorary Ambassador of the World Poets Federation; Honorary member of the Mozambican Writers Circle of the Diaspora (CEMD); Honorary member of the Lusophone International Movement (MIL); Honorary member of the "Unión Hispanomundial de Escritores UHE- Moçambique"; Honorary member of the ALDCI (Lusophone Association for Development, Culture and Integration)-ONGD; Lírio-Mor (International Culture distinction) in the Lírio Azul Movement (MLA); Commissioner of the Project "Ser Mulher" (To Be a Woman); Member of the Patripove Advisory Board; and Secretary of the Fiscal Council of Tricanas Poveiras

Elizabeth O. Ogunmodede
is a teenage Nigerian, living in Nigeria. She was born on the 31st day of August 2007. She is an award-winning poet, and author of a children's poetry book titled I LOVE TO GO TO SCHOOL, and author of the collection of stories titled LESSONS FROM GRANDMA. She is also a contributor to international poetry anthologies and she is a co-author of a poetry book titled WISDOM AND VOICES. Her works have appeared in some online literary magazines and publications. She loves reading fictional works and poems. She also loves music. Her Young Adult fiction novel titled Ladder to the top is on the verge of publishing.

Richard Ogunmodede
Richard O. Ogunmodede is a Nigerian poet and an author, he has contributed to poetry anthologies. And he's also into short story writing. He's an artisan who is based in Nigeria. He loves playing board games such as chess, scrabble, and monopoly.

Taofeek Ògúnpérí
Taofeek Ọlálékan Ògúnpérí is a Nigerian writer. He writes poems, essays, creative nonfiction, reviews, among others. He is the author of Twisted Tongues (ATMAN Limited, 2017) and two forthcoming poetry collections – Fourteen, which he compiled during COVID-19 lockdown; and Songs of the Tryst, a selection from his over 400 love poems written on his WhatsApp status. His works have appeared or forthcoming in many print and electronic literary platforms including but not limited to Kreative Diadem, The Scribe Post, ARKore Writes, Kwara Pulse, New York Parrot, Parkchester Times. He is a volunteer in community service programs. A multiple award-winning student, Taofeek studies Literature-in-English at the Department of English of Obafemi Awolowo University, Ile-Ife. He tweets via @TaofeekOgunperi and receives mail through ogunperitaofeek@gmail.com

Ngozi Olivia Osuoha
Ngozi Olivia Osuoha is a Nigerian poet/writer/thinker/author. She's a graduate of Estate Management with experience in Banking and Broadcasting. She has featured in over sixty international anthologies and has equally published over two hundred and sixty poems in over twenty five countries. She has authored twenty three poetry books and some of them are archived in the United States' Library of Congress. She is also a tailor. Some of her poems have been nominated for both the Best Of The Net Awards and Pushcart Prize. Some of her works have also been translated into and published in some languages, including Spanish, Arabic, Farsi, Macedonian, Russian, Romanian, Khloe, Polish, among others.

Francis Otole
Francis Otole is a Nigerian born poet and academician. A member of the Association of Nigerian Authors (ANA) and many other literary groups. He is an award winning poet from the local and international scenes. Has been featured in magazines, journals, and anthologies; locally and internationally. He is a graduate of the prestigious Benue State University and a student of life. His hobby is reading and writing. He is married with two children

Carlo Parcelli,
the Co-host of The Foreign Policy on NY Parrot TV, is a poet and poetry editor and native Washingtonian still residing in the Washington DC area. For 25 years, he was mentored by the James Joyce scholar, Dr. Rudd Fleming at the University of Maryland. His poetics borrow from Pound's Cantos and the monologue style of David Jones. He has published 6 books total and over a 55 year career has had dozens of poems and articles appear in journals and anthologies such Andre Codrescu's 'Exquisite Corpse', The Pearl, Jack

Hirschman's Revolutionary Poet's Brigade, Science as Culture, and the premier Ezra Pound journal, 'Make It New'. He is Beat Poet Laureate Emeritus for Maryland.

Monalisa Parida
Monalisa Parida is from India, Odisha is a post graduate in English literature and a prolific poetess. She's very active in social media platforms and her poems have also been published in various e-journals and translated into different languages. She has got 64 international award for writing poetry. She also got International Ambassador Of Peace award from " World Literary Forum For Peace and Human Rights, Bhutan."She has got Honorary Doctorate from "Global Alliance For Autism and Peo", Alexandria, Egypt. Her poems have been publishing international e-journals "New York parrot", "The Writers Club" (USA), "Suriyadoya literary foundation", "kabita Minar", "Indian Periodical" (India) and "Offline Thinker ", "The Gorkha Times " (Nepal), "The Light House"(Portugal), "Bharatvision"(Romania), "International cultural forum for humanity and creativity"(Aleppo, Syria), "Atunispoetry.com"(Singapore) etc. And also published in various newspapers like "The Punjabi Writer Weekly(USA)", "News Kashmir (J&K, India)", Republic of Sungurlu (Turkey)" etc. One of her poem published an American anthology named "The Literary Parrot Series-1(New York, USA)". Her poems have been translated in various languages like Hindi, Bengali, Turkish, Persian, Romanian etc.

Evie Petropoulou
Eva was born in Xylokastro where she completed her basics studies. She developed interest in journalism when she was young, and later studied journalism at the ANT1 School. In 1994 she worked as a journalist in French newspaper "Le LIBRE JOURNAL," but her love for Greece won, so returned to her sunny home. Since 2002, she has been living and working in Athens.She works as a web radio producer, reading fairy tales at radio logotexniko vima every Sunday. Recently, she became responsible for the children literary section in Vivlio anazitiseis publications in Cuprys. She published: " I and my other avenger, my Skia publications Saita." "Zeraldin and The elf of the lake" in Italian and in French as well as "The daughter of the Moon" in 2 languages English and Greek. The Moon Daughter published by Ocelotos 4 times, received best reviews for author's writing and writing style. She is a member of the UNESCO Logos and Art Group of the writers of Corinth, Panhellenic Writers Association. Also her work was mentioned in the popular Greek encyclopedia for Poets and authors, Harry Patsi, page 300. Her books have been approved by the Ministry of Education of Cyprus. Eva's recent work includes: "The water Amazon fairy called Myrtia" ,illustrated by Vivi Markatos, dedicated to a girl that became handicap after a sexual assault and the translation of stories of Lafcadio Hearn, "Fairytravel with stories from Far East", an idea illustrated by Ms Ntina Anastasiadoy, a well known sculptor and sumi e painter in Greece.

Claudia Piccinno
Claudia Piccinno was born in the south of Italy, but she lives and teaches in the north of Italy. Operating in more than 100 anthologies, she's a former member of the jury in many national and international literary prizes. She is the Continental Director for Europe in the World Festival Poetry, she represents Istanbul culture in Italy as Ambassador of Ist Sanat Art Association. She has published 38 poetry books, among her own poetry collections and other poets' translations into Italian language. She was conferred with the most prestigious award "Stele of Rosetta" in Istanbul in 2016, the Literary Awards Naji Naaman Prize 2018, "World icon for peace" for Wip in Ondo city, Nigeria, in April 2017; Global Icon Award 2020 for Writers Capital International Foundation, The light of Galata, Turkey 2021. She gained almost 250 prizes in Italy for poetry and cultural merits. Her poem "In Blue" is played on a majolica stele posted on the seafront in Santa Caterina di Nardo (Le). She is European editor for the international literary magazine Papirus in Turkey and for Atunis Magazine international. She was responsible for poetry

in the Italian magazine called Gazzetta of Istanbul, printed in Turkey by the Italian community. She writes for e- magazine and literature newspapers such as Menabò, Verbumpress, Il Porticciolo. Her website is https://claudiapiccinno.weebly.com

Jonathan Rizzo
Elban poet with a Parisian background and historical studies in Florence with a Master's thesis on Napoleon's exile on the island of Elba. Experience as a radio speaker on a web radio and host of an art and culture program for a web TV. He collaborates as artistic director and organizer of cultural events for various literary cafes in various cities of Italy. Poet performer. Sailor, gypsy.

LaVan Robinson,
born as Larry LaVan Richardson, Jr, took his pen name from his middle name and his mother Mary's maiden name. He writes in her honor. As well, he has a beloved son, Audy. LaVan is a 13-year veteran, he has written poetry since high school. "LaLa" is Robinson's poet name. He states that he loves poetry and will use it to inspire people and bring them closer to God. LaVan has 5 books of poetry available on Amazon as well as contributions to anthologies and literary journals. You can find LaLa performing at open mics and on podcasts. He can be found on Facebook, Instagram, and Twitter.

Amita Sanghavi
teaches at SQU in Oman. She completed M.A EngLit, B.ed,(University of Mumbai) M.Phil (SNDT University).She's recipient of British Council Hornby award and Dr.Colaco award and has an MA (TESOL) from Lancaster University, UK. She's pronounced Ambassador of Poetry by World Poetry, Canada and Representative of Immages&Poetry Art Movement, Italy. She won Savona International prize (2020), Italy. Her poetry book "Lavender Memories" and edited anthologies 'World Poetry Peaceathon' and 'Impressions & Expressions' were published in 2018, 2020, 2021.

Sankha Sen
Since childhood, Sen has always been good at his studies. The prizes, which he won for standing 1st in his classes, has been well preserved by his parents in Kolkata. Later on he graduated from a renowned Engineering University and started working in many countries. He did his Masters from a very good University in Germany and settled down there. Apart from his academic excellence, he has always been a great musician from Childhood. He has won many prizes for Music from his school days. His father is a well-known guitarist. He has played too in Television, Radio and in Recording Studios. Later on he went on pursuing his music and have done many shows in India, Japan, Germany and also in Switzerland. His childhood hobby "writing" has been well encouraged by his mother and his wife and he has again started writing poems. Within such a short span, his first book "Sonkhomonjori" has been published in International Book Fair, Kolkata, India and his poems has been published in a journal called "Setu" in the United States of America. Also his poem has been published in a magazine called "Icchedana" in Germany. This multitalented person has been well acknowledged by the Calcutta Journalist Club at his book inauguration event in International Book Fair in Kolkata, India. As one can see, Sankha Sen has become globally well-known and is getting eventually greater responses from different countries. Hence "Hawajan" has decided to publish another extraordinary book of his, comprising his feelings with poetic compositions of different shades of human emotions in three different languages.

Tali Cohen Shabtai
was born in Jerusalem, Israel, and is an international poet of high esteem with works translated into many languages. She is the author of three bilingual volumes of poetry, "Purple Diluted in a Black's Thick"(2007),

"Protest" (2012) and "Nine Years From You"(2018). A fourth volume is forthcoming in 2021. She has lived many years in Oslo, Norway, and in the U.S.A. Tali is known in her country as a very prominent as a poet with a special lyric, "she doesn't give herself easily, but subject to her own rules".

Robert Simon

lives with his daughter in North Georgia and is Professor of Spanish and Portuguese at Kennesaw State University. He has published numerous books, articles, and other relevant texts on mysticism and otherness in the poetries of Angola, Portugal, and Spain. His poetry expresses a wish to find a deeper, loving connection with the people around him through themes of love, loss, redemption, and the triumph of the sublime. Robert also studies oboe performance and moonlights as an oboist.

Anata Kumar Singh

Anata Kumar Singh studies English literature and linguistic at Ravenshaw University, Cuttack. He started his writing debut career in your quote app. He has worked on a lot of anthologies.

Pankhuri Sinha

Bilingual young poetess and story writer from India, Pankhuri Sinha has two books of poems published in English, 'Prison Talkies' and 'Dear Suzannah', and five collections in Hindi, two collections of stories published in Hindi called 'Koi-bhi-Din' and 'Kissa-e-Kohinoor' with Gyanpeeth, and two more coming soon. She has been published in many journals, anthologies, home and abroad. She has won many prestigious, national-international awards. Her script for the UGC documentary 'Cobra-God at Mercy', won the best film award in 1997. Her poems have been translated in over twenty two languages, She has also published her original poems in English in magazines and anthologies in India, in the UK and the USA, Romania, and the world over. She has set up an international group of poets called 'Poets Without Borders' and regularly organizes theme based poetry readings. She won the best correspondence prize for her short story in the first Chekhov literature festival, in Yalta, Crimea in 2019. She won the special jury award in the Premio International Poetry contest in Italy in January 2021. Most recently, she won the 'Sahitto Excellence in Literature' Award in Bangladesh on the 30th of April and 3rd prize for her poetry 'Chekhov in my Heart', in the category, geography of Chekhov's places. Her writing is dominated by themes of exile, immigration, gender equality and environmental concerns. After doing her BA from Delhi University, and PG diploma in Journalism, from Symbiosis Pune, Pankhuri did her Master's in history from SUNY Buffalo, and has an unfinished Ph.D. from the University of Calgary, Canada. She has worked in various positions as a journalist, lecturer and a content editor.

Howard F. Stein,

Ph.D. Professor Emeritus, Department of Family and Preventive Medicine, University of Oklahoma Health Sciences Center, Oklahoma City, OK USA. Stein is also Poet Laureate at High Plains Society for Applied Anthropology.

Paul Stroble

teaches philosophy and religious studies at Webster University in St. Louis. He has published twenty-two books, about half of which are Bible studies and study books of religious curriculum. Finishing Line Press has published four chapbooks and one full-length collection of my poems, with another full-length collection forthcoming this fall.

Sushant Thapa
(26 Feb, 1993) holds a Master's degree in English Literature from Jawaharlal Nehru University, New Delhi, India. He is a Nepalese poet from Biratnagar, Nepal, and is the author of two poetry collections, "The Poetic Burden and Other Poems", published by Authorspress, New Delhi, India, in 2020 and "Abstraction and Other Poems" published by Impspired in 2021 from England. His English poems are featured in Trouvaille Review, Litehouse Exophonic Magazine (Portugal), International Times (United Kingdom), New York Parrot (New York, USA), My Republica (Kathmandu, Nepal), The Kathmandu Post (Kathmandu, Nepal), Sahitto Bilingual Literary Magazine (Bangladesh), Indian Periodical (India), Ponder Savant (California, USA), Grey Thoughts (New Jersey, USA), The Gorkha Times (Kathmandu, Nepal), The Piker Press (USA), Lothlorien Poetry Journal (France), Offline Thinker (Kathmandu, Nepal), Sahitya Post (Kathmandu, Nepal), Atunis Poetry (Belgium), EKL Review (India), Harbinger Asylum (USA), Dumpster Fire Press (USA), Impspired Magazine (UK), Sindh Courier (Pakistan), Aksharang (Lalitpur, Nepal), Kabita Minar (Odisha, India), Suryodaya Literary Foundation (India), Visible Magazine, WILLIWASH (Nigeria), The Beatnik Cowboy (South Dakota, USA), Synchronized Chaos Journal (San Lorenzo, California, USA), Vscorpiozine's Blog (USA), Medusa's Kitchen and As It Ought To Be Magazine (USA). Four English poems written by Sushant have been translated into Uzbek (the language of Uzbekistan) and published in the online literary magazine, Nodirabegim of Uzbekistan. He has also been anthologized in three English poetry collections, entitled Pandemic Poetry 2020 and An Anthology of Poetry for Children. One of Sushant's poems has appeared in The Literary Parrot Anthology published by Transcendent Zero Press and New York Parrot, New York, USA. One of his poems, entitled "Festivities", has been included in schoolbook used to teach English to Grade 6 students in Nepal. Sushant has also written and published Flash Fictions and Short stories from Kitaab and Borderless Journal, Singapore. His three poems were translated in Latin American Spanish Language and published in the Magazine Trinando of Mexico.

Jerena Tobiasen
is a Canadian writer currently residing on the west coast of British Columbia. Although she was born in Vancouver, Canada, she spent most of her school years and early adult life in Calgary and Winnipeg, where her father's job in the oil industry took them. She has always loved storytelling and credits her parents for sharing their own love. "Each time we moved into a new community, we had to rely on each other until we made new friends. We played games, shared stories of our heritage, and wandered through local museums. The need to appreciate history was ingrained in me early." Jerena spent most of her working life in some area of law, and for a large portion of it, she was a single mom. Occasionally, she took a side-step into real estate, self-employment, even dabbling in undercover work, but always she returned to law. She retired at the end of 2015. Three weeks later, she began writing a story inspired, in part, by events that began to unfold in the early 1990s and had haunted her ever since. Her work morphed into The Prophecy, a 3-book saga including The Crest, The Emerald and The Destiny, all of which are available in print and e-book format. The Crest and The Emerald are also available in audiobook format. In 2020, The Prophecy won a Canada Book Award, the Independent Press Award Distinguished Favorite – Historical Fiction Series, and the Next Generation Indie Book Award Fiction Series Finalist. The Destiny is also a Readers' Favorite Bronze Medal winner.Jerena enhances her writing, thirst for knowledge and understanding of history by travelling to foreign lands, visiting museums and libraries, conducting interviews, and walking in the footsteps of her characters. Twice she accompanies WW2 veterans to the battlefields of Flanders, Dieppe and Normandy. In 2016, she travelled to Germany and Poland tracing the paths of The Prophecy's characters. In 2019, she travelled extensively through southern Europe, northern Africa, the Arctic, and the Middle East collecting data for a new three-book series inspired by the Rosebud Egg, which she first observed in the Fabergé Museum in St. Petersburg, Russia in 2018.

First drafts of her next series are now being edited, pending a character-driven journey to destinations yet to be experienced. Her short story – The Blue Boots – was shortlisted for the writers' contest sponsored by Surrey International Writers Conference 2018. A collection of her short stories and other writings can be found on her website jerenatobiasen.ca, which, she notes, needs a little work. "Programming and website maintenance are not my forté!" she says. Jerena is a proud member of The Writers Union of Canada, the Canadian Authors Association, the Federation of BC Writers, the Royal City Literary Arts Society and The Royal Canadian Legion.

J R (Judy) Turek,
Walt Whitman Birthplace 2019 Long Island Poet of the Year, Superintendent of Poetry for the LI Fair, 2020 Hometown Hero by the East Meadow Herald, Bards Laureate 2013-2015, is an internationally published poet, translated into Korean, Romanian, French, and Italian; editor, workshop leader, and 24 years as Moderator of the Farmingdale Creative Writing Group; she has 2 Pushcart Prize nominations and recipient of the Conklin Prize For Poetry. She was named a 2017 NYS Woman of Distinction. She is the author of Midnight on the Eve of Never, B is for Betwixt and Between, A is for Almost Anything, Imagistics, They Come And They Go, and most recent 24 in 24. She writes a poem a day for over 17 years. J R, The Purple Poet, lives on Long Island with her soul-mate husband, Paul, her dogs, and her extraordinarily extensive shoe collection.

Chika Udekwe
is indigenous to Igga community, Uzo-Uwani Local Government Area, Enugu State, Nigeria. He is a graduate of English Language and Literary Studies(B.Arts/Ed) from the prestigious University of Nigeria, Nsukka. He is a member of National Association of Students of English and Literary Studies (NASELS); Poets In Nigeria (PIN) and Poets Without Borders. Some of his poems have been homed in different international multilingual anthologies such as: Rendition of International Poetry, China(2020); Arcs Prose Poem, Iraq(2020); Save Africa, USA(2019); Complexion Based Discrimination: Global Insights, India(2018) and 84 Delicious Bottles for Wole Soyinka anthology of 2018, Nigeria. He is one of the Birland poets and Biafran activist. His native food poem, "Ọjà Ịgbale" was shortlisted among the top ten winning poems of Food Poetry Competition of Poets in Nigeria, 2020. He is the author of Songs for the Soul: a collection of poems(2019). A one time assistant-editor of Seer's Craft, a Departmental magazine, 2018. He was the 2nd Runner-up of Mr Njoku Solomon's Poetry Contest, Nigeria, 2018; 2nd Runner-up of Chief Saleh Sherima's Debate Contest, Nigeria, 2017. He is an award-winning poet whose favorite poets are mostly Africans by origin. Classical works of Shakespeare and metaphysical poetry of John Donne, P. B. Shelly, motivated him to scribble about nature and secularism.

Uche Francis Uwadinachi
A Nigerian spoken word artist, radio presenter and poet.

Amrita Valan
Indian poet and creative writer

Petros Kyriakou Veloudas
was born in Agrinio Greece in 1977, where he lives to this day. He received his degree in Greek culture at the School of Humanities of the Greek Open University in Patras. He has worked as a radio producer on local radio stations, while publishing his poems or humorous stories in the newspapers of the city of Agrinio of MACHITI ANAGELIA, THE NEWS OF AITOLOAKARNANIA PALMOS. He was a municipal councilor of the municipal community of Agrinio, specifically vice president of the city of

Agrinio from 2014 to 2019. He was a former member of the Panhellenic Writers 'Union and now an active member of the Writers' Union of Etoloakarnania. His poems are included in pan-Hellenic anthologies (published by NEA ARIADNE, anthology of poets-novelists of Etoloakarnania during the period 1821-2002. Together with his literary work he is included in the electronic encyclopedia of the Panhellenic Contributions by contemporary Greek writers. He is currently a member of the International Society of Greek Writers (DEEL). His literary distinctions are commendable in the first pan-Hellenic prose competition, he was awarded to 1000 Greek poets, he is a member of the International Society of Greek Writers (DEEL).

Julene Tripp Weaver
is a psychotherapist and writer in Seattle. Her third poetry book, *truth be bold—Serenading Life & Death in the Age of AIDS*, was a finalist for a *Lambda Literary Award*, won the *Bisexual Book Award* and four *Human Relations Indie Book Awards*. Her work is widely published. Recent anthologies include: *Covid, Isolation & Hope: Artists Respond to the Pandemic*, and the upcoming, *Poets Speaking to Poets: Echoes and Tributes*. From her memoir writing, two essays are in the anthology, *But You Don't Look Sick: The Real Life Adventures of Fibro Bitches, Lupus Warriors, and other Super Heroes Battling Invisible Illness*. Find her at at www.julenetrippweaver.com, or on Twitter @trippweavepoet.

Kari Wergeland
Wergeland's poetry has appeared in many journals and anthologies, including Catamaran Literary Reader, Chariton Review, The MacGuffin, and The Main Street Rag. Her chapbook, Breast Cancer: A Poem in Five Acts, was named an Eric Hoffer Book Award category finalist in 2018. Meanwhile, her long library career has taken her into libraries up and down the West Coast. At some point in all of this, she served as a children's book reviewer for The Seattle Times.

John Yamrus
In a career spanning more than 50 years as a working writer, John Yamrus has published 28 volumes of poetry, 2 novels, 3 volumes of non-fiction and a children's book. He has also had more than 2,500 poems published in magazines and anthologies around the world. Selections of his work have been translated into several languages, including Spanish, Swedish, French, Japanese, Italian, Romanian, Albanian, Estonian and Bengali. His poetry is taught in numerous colleges and universities.

S. A. Yitta
is a Nigerian freelance journalist, poet, and university lecturer based in East Africa. He has numerous academic and non-academic publications locally and internationally.

Ewa Zelenay
poet, journalist, writer. Head Board member Polish Literates Union. Graduate in journalism and cultural research. Air and space are subjects for many of her poems. She spend many years in the sky - working Polish National Air Carrier LOT as flight attendant. Awards winner for more than twenty of literature competitions in Poland, including prestige priest / Jan Twardowski / competition for the most interesting volume of poetry in 2007. Painter, sculptor, photographer - in her work apply many technics that she call "IMPULSJONIZM" what generate her creations. Currently Ewa Zelenay cooperate with Polish National Radio Broadcasting Network also with Family One Program / radio theatre/ She continue write ; movies screenplays, show texts and song lyrics - that has been presented on stages by artists in Poland and abroad. Many of Ewa Zelenay poems were translated into English, Chinese, French, Italian, Hungarian, Telugu

and in incorporate in variety of anthologies and literature magazines and others. Ewa Maria Zelenay is also a juror of literary competitions and conducts lectures and poetry workshops.

ABOUT THE EDITORS

Dustin Pickering
is founder of Transcendent Zero Press and editor at Harbinger Asylum. He has published reviews at World Literature Today, Colorado Review, Huffington Post, and Cafe Dissensus.

Mutiu Olawuyi
Mutiu Olawuyi (popularly called the Jungle Poet) is the Executive Director of NY Parrot TV and producer of the only daily TV show on earth for creative writers/artists called The Literary Corner. He's an international award-winning poet - 2012 International Who's Who in Poetry Awardee, USA; 2013 World Poetry Empowered Poet Awardee, Canada, Honorary Professor - International Art Academy, Greece, and 2014 Marqui's Who's Who in the World Listee, USA, World Poetry Cultural Ambassador (2014) and the first recipient of World Poetry Conference Award of Poetry in Journalism (2021, India). He was the producer and host of ArtFlakes on CBA TV, the Voice of East Africa and also the Editor-in-Chief of Parkchester Times, New York Parrot and MCR newspapers (Print and Online) based in New York City, USA. He has authored numerous books of poetry (Among them are American Literary Legends and Other Poems [2010], Thoughts from the Jungle [2012], 9/11 Poetry [2012], The Journey to the Archangels [2013], etcetera) and has edited numerous international anthologies, academic journals and magazines. Mutiu is an edupreneur, freelance journalist/writer/editor, literary critic and inventor of a new form of poetry called 9eleven (a poem of 9 lines written with 11 syllables). He has some of his poems, short stories and research papers published in online and offline journals and magazines in India, Ireland, England, Canada, Greece, Nigeria and USA. Finally, some of his works have been translated to Arabic, French, Esperantos, Portuguese, Hindu, Igala, Yoruba, Hausa, Bengal, Polish, Nepali, Russian, Spanish, Swedish, Dutch, Italian and Hungarian. Contact Mutiu at editor@newyorkparrot.com

EPILOGUE BY MUTIU OLAWUYI

When the Parrots Talk

Even in cage, they muse their tongues
And sometimes dance to lyrical gongs
And mimic to store some codes beyond
thy thoughts – all for them to strengthen bond…
At Literary Corner, some parrots muse;
They muse their pains with no abuse
with poems, prose, plays and paints,
Weaving their words to mend the dents…
When the Parrot talks, the world is mute
as ears capture the codes to boot;
to boost the minds of "leads" and "leds"
and shape our *hands* and *hearts,* and *heads*…
We hope you read and cull wisdoms,
to live with ease –in both kingdoms…

www.ingramcontent.com/pod-product-compliance
Lightning Source LLC
Chambersburg PA
CBHW080515090426
42734CB00015B/3065